THE BOOK OF

LIGHT
DESSERTS

THE BOOK OF

LIGHT
DESSERTS

ANNE SHEASBY

Photographed by
JON STEWART

HPBooks
a division of
PRICE STERN SLOAN
Los Angeles

ANOTHER BEST SELLING VOLUME FROM HPBOOKS

HPBooks
A division of Price Stern Sloan, Inc.
11150 Olympic Boulevard
Suite 650
Los Angeles, CA 90064

9 8 7 6 5 4 3 2 1

ISBN 1-55788-086-7

By arrangement with Salamander Books Ltd.

Home Economists: Kerenza Harries and Jo Craig
Printed in Belgium by Proost International Book Production

CONTENTS

INTRODUCTION

A cookbook on the subject of light desserts probably seems like a contradiction in terms. How can a dessert be light and low in calories and fat, yet still be appealing and delectable to taste?

Nowadays, however, with the enormous range fresh fruits and natural foods readily available, it is easy to create healthy desserts which are light and attractive, too.

The desserts in this book will appeal to everyone. Although the calorie and fat contents of each recipe vary, they are all mouth-watering light desserts. Most of the recipes are economical, as well as being quick and easy to make. Special occasion desserts require slightly more costly ingredients and take longer to prepare, but they are well worth the extra effort.

Recipes include classic desserts, children's favorites, everyday delights and unusual exotic desserts, each one beautifully illustrated in full color and with step-by-step instructions.

Enjoy all these tempting desserts, while cutting down on your calorie and fat intakes, and the chances are you won't even notice the difference!

INGREDIENTS

Nowadays, healthy eating plays a vital role in our general well-being and adopting good eating habits is important.

The word 'dessert' conjures up a glorious picture of a delightful finale to complement any enjoyable meal. Light desserts can be just as tempting and delicious as the more fattening versions by making a few simple changes to the ingredients.

All the low-fat and low calorie ingredients used in the recipes in this book are readily and widely available, so you won't have to venture very far to find them.

MILK
Milk is a nutritious food and provides a good source of protein as well as many vitamins and minerals. It is an important ingredient in some of the recipes but instead of whole milk, either skimmed milk or low-fat milk has been used.

Skimmed milk contains all the protein and minerals of whole milk with the exception of the fat-soluble vitamins.

Low-fat milk contains either one or two percent butterfat, but retains all the protein and minerals of whole milk.

Evaporated milk is canned milk which has had a large percentage of its water content removed. It contains no added sugar and is a rich source of vitamin D. Reduced-fat evaporated milk is used in some of the recipes. It is particularly good for light desserts as it contains less than half the fat content of ordinary evaporated milk.

YOGURT
Yogurt is a delicious food which is often served on its own or as an accompaniment to other foods.

Natural yogurt has a slightly acidic but refreshing flavor that is excellent in all kinds of low-fat desserts. Both low-fat and nonfat natural yogurt are widely available. Use plain yogurt unless the recipe calls for a particular flavored yogurt.

CREAMS
Cream is an ingredient commonly associated with desserts. In the recipes in this book, light cream or half and half and light whipping cream are sometimes used in small amounts to add an extra richness and body to a dessert.

SOFT CHEESE
Both low-fat and nonfat cream cheese are widely available and can be used in making desserts to reduce the calories from fat. Cottage cheese has been used in some of the recipes and this is an excellent low-fat ingredient for desserts such as cheesecakes.

LOW FAT SPREAD
Some fat is essential in our diet, but fats such as butter, hard margarine, lard and suet should be avoided as much as possible. In place of regular butter or margarine which contain mostly fat, reduced-fat spread has been used as an alternative.

Low-fat spread generally contains half the fat of butter or margarine and is suitable for baking, melting and pastry-making.

SUGAR
Sugar is high in calories but contains few nutrients, so for good health we should cut down on sugar in our diet as much as possible.

Three types of sugar have been used in these light dessert recipes – granulated sugar, brown sugar and powdered sugar, each having its own characteristic flavor.

HONEY
In some recipes honey has been used in place of sugar. Honey is naturally sweeter than sugar, so less needs to be used in recipes. It also has a pleasant taste of its own.

FLOUR
In some of the recipes, whole-wheat flour has been used. It contains more dietary fiber than white flour, making it a healthier alternative, and has a delicious flavor too.

FRUIT
Fruit is a ready source of energy. Vitamins and minerals are present in most fruits as well as natural fruit sugar or fructose. Most fruits are low in calories.

Fresh, canned or dried fruit can be put to numerous uses in the kitchen, in sweet and savory dishes, and fruit forms an important ingredient in many of these light desserts.

The natural sugar and acids found in fruit contribute to the flavor and texture of the dessert and many fruits are a good source of fiber, particularly if their edible skins are left on when they are used in desserts.

Choose fresh, plump, firm fruits avoiding wrinkled, moldy or bruised fruits as these will spoil the flavor of the dessert. Many fruits are available all year round nowadays, but canned and frozen fruits make excellent substitutes at times when fresh fruits are unavailable.

Always remember to wash and dry any fresh fruit before using it in a dessert.

Dried fruit is sweeter and richer than fresh fruit and is excellent for light desserts. Dried fruit is an excellent source of fiber, full of concentrated flavor and nutrients.

NUTS
Nuts are a good source of energy, high in protein, carbohydrates and fat which means they are high in calories too!

Chopped and ground nuts have been used in some of the recipes to add texture and flavor but the quantities have been kept fairly low.

CAROB
Carob can be used in place of chocolate or cocoa. Carob, produced from the carob bean, is available in chips, bar or powder form. It is naturally sweeter than chocolate although lower in calories and free from caffeine.

Remember to sieve the carob powder (or carob flour as it may be called) thoroughly before using it in any of the desserts.

SUGAR-FREE FLAVORED GELATINS
Sugar-free flavored gelatins make an ideal addition to some light dessert recipes, adding flavor while reducing both the sugar and calorie content of a dessert.

> The serving suggestion, such as custard, yogurt, etc., at the end of most recipes is not included in the calories counts and fat figures. Grams of fat have been rounded to the nearest whole number.

RASPBERRY BAVARIAN

1 (14-oz.) can raspberries packed in fruit juice
1 (1/2-oz.) package sugar-free raspberry gelatin
1-3/4 cups reduced-fat evaporated milk, chilled
Fresh raspberries and mint sprigs, to decorate

Drain raspberries over a bowl, reserving juice. Add enough water to juice to make 1-1/4 cups.

In a saucepan over low heat, stir juice mixture and gelatin. When gelatin dissolves, remove from heat and set aside to cool. In a large bowl, beat evaporated milk until thick. Add raspberries and cooled gelatin mixture and mix well.

Pour mixture into a glass serving bowl. Cover and refrigerate until set. Turn out mold onto a serving plate. Decorate with raspberries and mint sprigs before serving.

Makes 6 to 8 servings.

Total calories: 914   Total fat: 18 g
Calories per serving: 152   Fat per serving: 3 g

MUESLI CHEESECAKE

3 tablespoons reduced-fat margarine, melted
1-1/4 cups sugar-free muesli
1 tablespoon unflavored gelatin powder
3 tablespoons water
1-1/2 cups low-fat cream cheese
1/4 cup sugar
Grated peel and juice of 1 lemon
2/3 cup light whipping cream
Fresh fruit, to decorate, such as strawberries, figs, and
    peaches

In a bowl, mix margarine with muesli. Press mixture over bottom of an 8-inch springform pan. Refrigerate until chilled.

Sprinkle gelatin over water in a small bowl. Set aside 2 to 3 minutes to soften. Stand bowl in a saucepan of hot water and stir until gelatin has dissolved. Cool slightly. In a bowl, beat cream cheese, sugar, lemon peel, and juice together. Stir in dissolved gelatin. In a separate bowl, whip cream lightly. Fold into cream cheese mixture.

Pour mixture over muesli crust, leveling surface. Return to the refrigerator to set. To serve, remove cheesecake from pan, place on a serving plate and decorate with fresh fruit.

Makes 6 servings.

Total calories: 1467   Total fat: 63 g
Calories per serving: 245   Fat per serving: 10 g

MOCHA POTS

1 tablespoon cornstarch
2/3 cup skim milk
1/4 cup sugar
3 ounces semisweet chocolate, broken into pieces
1/2 teaspoon instant coffee granules
1 tablespoon warm water
1-1/4 cups nonfat yogurt
Kumquat slices and chocolate sprinkles, to decorate

In a saucepan, blend cornstarch with milk. Add sugar and chocolate and cook over low heat, stirring constantly, until mixture thickens. Cook 3 minutes, then cool slightly.

In a small bowl, dissolve coffee in warm water. When chocolate mixture is cool, stir in coffee and yogurt until thoroughly combined.

Spoon mixture into individual glass serving dishes. Cover and refrigerate before serving. When ready to serve, decorate each dessert with kumquat slices and chocolate sprinkles.

Makes 4 servings.

Total calories: 923   Total fat: 25 g
Calories per serving: 231   Fat per serving: 6 g

Note: If kumquats are not available, orange slices can be used as decoration.

— BAKED APPLES WITH PRUNES —

4 large apples, such as MacIntosh
1 cup finely chopped dried prunes
4 teaspoons honey
2 teaspoons apple-pie spice
1/4 cup water
Nonfat yogurt, low-fat custard or whipped cream with
   ground cinnamon, to serve

Preheat oven to 350F (175C). Wash and dry apples, but do not peel. Using an apple corer, remove apple cores. Using a small knife, make a shallow cut through the skin around each apple.

Stand apples in a baking dish. Fill apple cavities with prunes, pushing them down firmly. Top with honey and sprinkle each apple with apple pie spice.

Pour water around apples. Bake apples 45 to 60 minutes or until soft. Serve hot with nonfat yogurt.

Makes 4 servings.

Total calories: 538   Total fat: 34 g
Calories per serving: 135   Fat per serving: 0.4 g

Variation: Dried figs may be used in place of prunes.

RED FRUIT MEDLEY

1/2 cup sugar
1-3/4 cup water
1/2 pound strawberries
1/2 pound cherries
8 red plums
2 Red Delicious apples
1/2 pound raspberries
Fresh mint, to decorate
Nonfat yogurt, to serve

Into a saucepan, place sugar and water. Cook over low heat, stirring occasionally, until sugar dissolves. Boil rapidly, uncovered, 10 minutes. Set aside to cool.

To prepare fruit, cut strawberries in half and pit cherries. Halve and pit plums. Core apples and cut into chunks. Place all the fruit into a large serving bowl.

Pour cooled sugar mixture over fruit and stir gently to mix. Refrigerate until chilled before serving. Decorate with mint and serve with yogurt.

Makes 6 servings.

Total calories: 923   Total fat: 2 g
Calories per serving: 154   Fat per serving: 0.3 g

LIME CHEESE MOLD

1 (1/2-oz.) package sugar-free lime gelatin
1 cup boiling water
1 cup cold water
1 cup low-fat cream cheese
Grated peel and juice of 1 lime
Lemon and lime slices, to decorate

In a saucepan over low heat, dissolve gelatin in 1 cup boiling water. Add 1 cup cold water. Set aside to cool.

In a blender or food processor, blend together cooled gelatin mixture, cream cheese and lime peel and juice. Pour mixture into a dampened 3-1/4-cup mold. Cover and refrigerate until set.

When ready to serve, unmold dessert onto a serving plate. Decorate with lemon and lime slices.

Makes 4 servings.

Total calories: 654	Total fat: 15 g
Calories per serving: 164	Fat per serving: 3.8 g

Variation: Use a lemon-flavored gelatin and lemon peel and juice for a slightly different taste.

—CHERRY YOGURT SYLLABUB—

1 (14-oz.) can cherries
2 cups nonfat cherry yogurt
2/3 cup dry white wine
2/3 cup light whipping cream
Ladyfingers, to serve

Drain cherries, then remove pits.

In a blender or food processor, blend together yogurt, wine and cherries. In a medium-size bowl, whip cream until thick. Gradually fold cream into the fruit mixture.

Spoon cherry mixture into 6 individual glasses. Cover and refrigerate at least 2 hours before serving. Serve with ladyfingers.

Makes 6 servings.

Total calories: 1158   Total fat: 39 g
Calories per serving: 193   Fat per serving: 6.5 g

Variation: Reserve a few of the cherries for decoration.

LEMON FRUIT KABOBS

1 small pineapple
3 kiwifruit
1/2 small melon
2 peaches
12 large strawberries
Grated peel and juice of 1 lemon
1 tablespoon cornstarch
2 tablespoons sugar
Lime slices, to decorate (optional)

To prepare fruit, cut pineapple into thick slices, then peel and discard core. Cut flesh into chunks.

Peel kiwifruit, then cut into quarters. Peel and remove seeds from melon and cut flesh into chunks. Peel and pit peaches, then cut into chunks. Halve strawberries. Thread fruit onto 12 kabob skewers. Place on a serving dish, cover with plastic wrap and refrigerate. To make sauce, in a measuring cup, add enough water to lemon juice to make 1-1/4 cups.

In a saucepan, blend cornstarch and sugar with lemon juice mixture. Add grated lemon peel. Bring to a boil, stirring constantly, until mixture thickens. Cook 3 minutes longer, stirring. Serve hot lemon sauce immediately with fruit kabobs. Serve 2 kabobs per person and garnish each serving with lime slices, if desired.

Makes 6 servings.

Total calories: 660   Total fat: 3 g
Calories per serving: 110   Fat per serving: 0.5 g

GRAPEFRUIT-YOGURT SUNDAES

9 semisweet whole-wheat cookies
1/4 cup reduced-fat margarine, melted
3 cups bran flakes
1 (14-oz.) can grapefruit in fruit juice, drained and
    finely chopped
1-1/4 cups low-fat plain yogurt
Grapefruit sections and mint sprigs, to decorate

Crush cookies to crumbs, then mix with melted margarine and bran flakes.

In a bowl, mix together grapefruit and yogurt. Layer yogurt mixture and crunch mixture in 6 glass dishes, finishing with a crunch layer.

Cover and refrigerate until ready to serve. Decorate desserts with grapefruit sections and mint sprigs.

Makes 6 servings.

Total calories: 1200   Total fat: 43 g
Calories per serving: 200   Fat per serving: 7 g

Variation: Substitute other crunchy types of cereal for bran flakes.

ORANGE FLUFF

1 (1/2-oz.) package sugar-free orange gelatin
1 cup boiling water
1 cup cold water
3/4 cup reduced-fat evaporated milk, chilled
1 cup low-fat cream cheese, room temperature
Tangerine segments and mint sprigs, to decorate

In a medium-size bowl, dissolve gelatin in boiling water. Stir in cold water. Set aside until just beginning to set.

In a bowl, whip evaporated milk until thick. In another bowl, place cream cheese and beat until smooth. Gradually beat evaporated milk into cream cheese until thoroughly combined. Fold gelatin into the cream cheese mixture until evenly mixed.

Pour mixture into a dampened 3-3/4 cup mold. Cover and refrigerate until set. When ready to serve, unmold onto a serving dish. Decorate with tangerine segments and mint sprigs.

Makes 4 servings.

Total calories: 568   Total fat: 23 g
Calories per serving: 142   Fat per serving: 6 g

PEACH TRIFLE

3 tablespoons reduced-sugar strawberry jam
5 slices pound cake
1 (14-oz.) can peach slices packed in fruit juice
2 tablespoons sweet sherry
1 (1/2-oz.) package sugar-free strawberry gelatin
1 cup boiling water
1-1/4 cups cold water
1 tablespoon cornstarch
1 tablespoon sugar
Pinch of salt
3 egg yolks
2 cups skim milk
2/3 cup light whipping cream, lightly whipped
Fresh fruit, to decorate

Spread jam on cake; cut into fingers.

Place in a glass serving dish. Drain peaches, reserving juice. Mix together peach juice and sherry and pour over cake. Arrange peach slices over cake. Dissolve gelatin in boiling water, then stir in cold water. Cool and then pour gelatin mixture over cake. Cover and refrigerate until set. Meanwhile, to make custard, blend cornstarch, sugar, salt and egg yolks with 3 tablespoons milk. In a saucepan, heat remaining milk until hot, then pour over cornstarch mixture, stirring well.

Return mixture to saucepan and bring to a boil, stirring, until thickened. Boil 1 minute, stirring. Pour into a bowl to cool, covered with a damp cloth. When cool, spread it over gelatin; top with cream and fruit.

Makes 6 servings.

Total calories: 1479   Total fat: 62 g
Calories per serving: 246   Fat per serving: 10 g

Variation: Sprinkle chopped nuts over the top, but remember this adds calories.

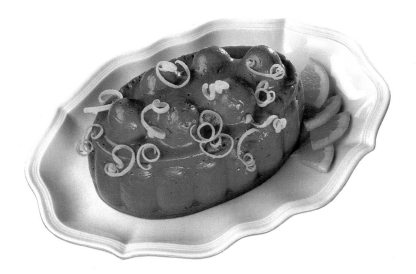

-CHOC-ORANGE BLANCMANGE-

1/4 cup cornstarch
3 tablespoons sugar
2-1/2 cups skim milk
4 ounces semisweet chocolate chips
Grated peel of 1 large orange
Orange slices and peel, to decorate

In a bowl, blend cornstarch and sugar with 2 tablespoons of the milk. In a saucepan, heat remaining milk and chocolate chips together until milk is hot and chocolate melts, stirring.

Pour chocolate mixture over cornstarch mixture, stirring well. Return mixture to saucepan and bring to a boil, stirring constantly until mixture thickens. Cook 3 minutes longer, stirring. Stir in orange peel. Pour into a dampened 3-cup mold and refrigerate until ready to serve.

When ready to serve, turn out mold onto a serving plate. Decorate with orange slices and peel.

Makes 6 servings.

Total calories: 1159   Total fat: 34 g
Calories per serving: 193   Fat per serving: 6 g

Note: To unmold the dessert; immerse the mold in hot water 2 to 3 seconds and place a damp serving plate on top of mold. Hold in position and quickly invert together.

FIVE FRUIT SALAD

1/2 melon
2 Red Delicious apples
12 fresh dates
6 ounces seedless green grapes
1 (14-oz.) can apricot halves packed in fruit juice
1-3/4 cups tropical fruit juice

To prepare fruit, peel and remove seeds from melon. Cut flesh into chunks. Core apples and cut into chunks.

Halve and pit dates. Halve grapes, if they are large in size. Drain apricots, reserving juice. Place all fruit in a large glass serving dish.

Mix reserved apricot juice with tropical fruit juice, pour over fruit and stir gently to mix. Cover and leave to stand in a cool place 2 to 3 hours before serving.

Makes 6 servings.

Total calories: 815   Total fat: 1.9 g
Calories per serving: 136   Fat per serving: 0.3 g

APPLE & GINGER CRISP

1 pound cooking apples
2 tablespoons water
2 tablespoons brown sugar
1/4 cup reduced-fat margarine
2 tablespoons honey
2 cups rolled oats
2 teaspoons ground ginger
Low-fat custard, to serve

Preheat oven to 350F (175C). Peel, core and slice apples. Into a saucepan, place apple slices and water. Cook over low heat until apples have softened, stirring occasionally.

Stir in sugar and remove from heat. Spoon stewed apples into a 5-cup baking dish. Set aside. In a saucepan, melt margarine and honey together. Remove from heat and stir in oats and ginger until thoroughly combined.

Place oat mixture on top of apples. Bake 30 minutes or until brown and crispy on top. Serve hot or cold with custard sauce.

Makes 6 servings.

Total calories: 1200   Total fat: 36 g
Calories per serving: 200   Fat per serving: 6 g

—— PLUM & APPLE MOUSSES ——

12 ounces cooking apples
12 ounces plums
2 tablespoons lemon juice
5 tablespoons water
1 tablespoon unflavored gelatin powder
1/4 cup honey
1-1/4 cups low-fat plain yogurt
Apple slices and mint sprigs, to decorate

Peel, core and slice apples. Halve and pit plums. Into a saucepan, put apple slices and plum halves with lemon juice and 2 tablespoons of the water. Cover and cook over low heat until soft, stirring occasionally.

Remove from heat and cool slightly. In a blender or food processor, puree fruit. Cool completely. In a small bowl, sprinkle gelatin over remaining 3 tablespoons water. Set aside 2 to 3 minutes to soften. Stand bowl in a saucepan of hot water and stir until gelatin dissolves. Cool slightly.

Stir dissolved gelatin into plum-and-apple mixture. Stir in honey and yogurt; mix together well. Spoon mixture into individual glass serving dishes. Refrigerate until set. Decorate with apple slices and mint sprigs.

Makes 4 servings.

Total calories: 605   Total fat: 3 g
Calories per serving: 151   Fat per serving: 0.7 g

——— POACHED NECTARINES ———

2-1/2 cups unsweetened apple juice
1/3 cup sugar
Pared peel of 1 lemon
1 cinnamon stick
8 whole cloves
4 nectarines
1/4 cup sliced almonds, toasted

In a saucepan, mix together apple juice, sugar, lemon peel, cinnamon stick and cloves. To peel nectarines, dip into boiling water about 15 seconds, then plunge into a bowl of cold water. With a sharp knife carefully peel off skins.

To juice mixture in saucepan, add nectarines as soon as they are peeled to prevent discoloring. Over high heat, bring mixture to a boil. Reduce heat to low, cover and simmer 5 to 10 minutes, shaking pan occasionally. Spoon nectarines and juice mixture into a heatproof container. Cool, then cover and refrigerate overnight.

Remove cinnamon stick, peel, and cloves, if desired, from the juice before serving. To serve, place nectarines and some juice in individual dishes and sprinkle each nectarine with almonds.

Makes 4 servings.

Total calories: 942   Total fat: 15 g
Calories per serving: 236   Fat per serving: 4 g

Variation: If nectarines are not available, use peaches instead.

——— BLACKBERRY SUPREME ———

1 pound blackberries
1/4 cup sugar
5 tablespoons water
1 tablespoon unflavored gelatin powder
1-3/4 cups low-fat plain yogurt
Fresh blackberries and mint sprigs, to decorate

Into a saucepan, place blackberries and sugar with 2 tablespoons of the water. Cook over low heat until blackberries have softened, stirring occasionally. Set aside to cool.

In a small bowl, sprinkle gelatin over remaining 3 tablespoons water. Set aside 2 to 3 minutes to soften. Stand bowl in a saucepan of hot water and stir until gelatin dissolves. Cool slightly.

In a blender or food processor, puree together blackberries, gelatin and yogurt until well mixed. Pour into a large serving dish, cover and refrigerate until set. Decorate with fresh blackberries and mint sprigs before serving.

Makes 4 servings.

Total calories: 884   Total fat: 35 g
Calories per serving: 221   Fat per serving: 9 g

—— CITRUS FRUIT COCKTAIL ——

6 oranges
2 pink grapefruit
1 white grapefruit
8 kumquats
1-3/4 cups freshly squeezed orange juice
3 tablespoons honey
Grated peel of 1 lime
Shredded lemon or lime peel, to decorate

To prepare fruit, cut off peel and pith from oranges and grapefruit.

Holding fruit over a bowl, using a sharp knife, cut out segments from between membranes and place in the bowl. Squeeze membranes over bowl to extract juice. Wipe and thinly slice kumquats crosswise. Place in bowl.

In a measuring cup, mix together orange juice, honey and grated lime peel. Pour over fruit in the bowl and mix gently to combine. Place in a serving dish and refrigerate until chilled before serving. Spoon into individual glass bowls and sprinkle with shredded peel.

Makes 4 servings.

Total calories: 920   Total fat: 3 g
Calories per serving: 230   Fat per serving: 0.7 g

—RASPBERRY-APPLE STREUSEL—

1 pound cooking apples
2 tablespoons water
12 ounces raspberries
1/2 cup packed brown sugar
1/3 cup reduced-fat margarine
3/4 cup whole-wheat flour
1 cup rolled oats
1 teaspoon ground cinnamon
Low-fat custard sauce, to serve (optional)

Preheat oven to 400F (205C). Peel, core and slice apples. Into a saucepan, place apple slices and water. Cook over low heat until just softened, stirring occasionally.

Stir in raspberries and 2 tablespoons of the sugar. Into a 5-cup baking dish, place apple mixture, reserving any excess juice. In a bowl, rub or cut in margarine into remaining sugar and flour until mixture resembles coarse crumbs. Stir in oats and cinnamon.

Spoon streusel mixture over fruit and press down lightly. Bake 35 to 40 minutes or until streusel is golden and crisp. Serve hot or cold with custard sauce, if desired.

Makes 6 servings.

Total calories: 1455
Calories per serving: 243

Total fat: 42 g
Fat per serving: 7 g

—RHUBARB & ORANGE FOOLS—

2 pounds rhubarb, cut into 1-inch pieces
6 tablespoons unsweetened orange juice
5 tablespoons strawberry jam
2 tablespoons honey
2/3 cup light whipping cream
1-1/4 cups nonfat plain yogurt
Orange slices and mint sprigs, to decorate
Sugar cookies, to serve (optional)

Into a saucepan, put rhubarb with orange juice, jam and honey. Bring to a boil, then cover and simmer until rhubarb is soft and pulpy, stirring occasionally.

Cool slightly, then, in a blender or food processor, puree rhubarb. Transfer puree into a bowl and cool completely. In a separate bowl, whip cream lightly. Fold cream and yogurt into cooled rhubarb mixture.

Spoon mixture into 6 individual glasses and refrigerate until ready to serve. Decorate each dessert with orange slices and mint sprigs, and serve with sugar cookies, if desired.

Makes 6 servings.

Total calories: 1066   Total fat: 60 g
Calories per serving: 178   Fat per serving: 10 g

—— RICE & HONEY DESSERT ——

3 tablespoons cornstarch
1-1/2 cups skim milk
1/4 cup short-grain white rice
3 tablespoons honey
Unsweetened cocoa powder, to decorate
Strawberries, to serve (optional)

In a large bowl, blend cornstarch with 2 tablespoons milk; set aside. In a saucepan over low heat, bring remaining milk, rice and honey to a boil. Cover and simmer 30 minutes or until rice is soft, stirring occasionally.

Pour hot rice mixture over cornstarch mixture, stirring well. Return mixture to saucepan and cook, stirring, until mixture thickens. Cook, stirring, 3 minutes longer. Pour mixture into 6 (1/2-cup) dampened molds.

Cool slightly, then refrigerate dessert until ready to serve. To serve, invert onto a dampened serving dish, turn out of mold (page 21). Sift cocoa powder over desserts. Serve with strawberries, if desired.

Makes 4 servings.

Total calories: 683   Total fat: 30 g
Calories per serving: 171   Fat per serving: 0.7 g

Note: Pour the mixture into a 3-cup mold, if preferred.

——————— BAKEWELL TART ———————

2 cups self-rising flour
1/2 cup reduced-fat margarine
4 tablespoons reduced-sugar raspberry jam
1/4 cup granulated sugar
1 egg, beaten
3 tablespoons ground blanched almonds
1 teaspoon almond extract
2 tablespoons powdered sugar
1 tablespoon water

Preheat oven to 350F (175C). Sift 1 cup of the flour into a bowl. Rub or cut in 1/4 cup of the margarine until mixture resembles coarse crumbs.

Stir in about 2 tablespoons water or enough to make a soft dough. On a lightly floured surface, roll out dough to a 10-inch circle, then use to line an 8-inch quiche dish. With a fork, prick bottom of dough. Line with foil and fill with dried beans or pie weights. Bake 10 minutes. Remove foil and beans. Cool pastry slightly, then spread with raspberry jam. In a bowl, cream together remaining margarine and sugar. Gradually beat in egg. Fold in remaining flour, ground almonds and extract. Spoon over jam, leveling surface. Bake 25 minutes or until browned.

In a small bowl, mix powdered sugar with water. Spread mixture over tart while it is still warm. Serve warm or cold.

Makes 8 servings.

Total calories: 1980   Total fat: 82 g
Calories per serving: 248   Fat per serving: 10 g

QUICK CHERRY BRULEE

1 (14-oz.) can sweet cherries packed in syrup
1-1/4 cups low-fat plain yogurt
1/3 cup packed brown sugar
Mint sprigs, to decorate

Preheat broiler. Drain and pit cherries. Arrange cherries in a 3-3/4-cup baking dish.

Spread yogurt over cherries. Sprinkle sugar over the yogurt, covering it completely.

Place dish under broiler; broil until sugar becomes dark and bubbling. Let cool, then refrigerate 2 to 3 hours before serving. Decorate with mint sprigs.

Makes 4 servings.

Total calories: 720   Total fat: 4 g
Calories per serving: 180   Fat per serving: 1 g

—LOGANBERRY LAYER DESSERT—

1/2 pound loganberries or raspberries
2 tablespoons water
1/2 cup light whipping cream
2-1/2 cups nonfat yogurt
1/2 cup powdered sugar, sifted
Fresh loganberries and mint sprigs, to decorate

In a saucepan, place loganberries and water. Simmer until just softened, stirring occasionally. Cool slightly, then in a blender or food processor, puree. Cool completely. In a bowl, whip cream until thick.

In a separate bowl, gently stir together pureed loganberries, half of the cream, half of the yogurt and half of the sugar. In another bowl, gently stir together remaining cream, yogurt and sugar.

Into 6 glasses, layer loganberry mixture and yogurt mixture, beginning and ending with a berry layer. Cover and refrigerate until ready to serve. Decorate desserts with fresh loganberries and mint sprigs before serving.

Makes 6 servings.

Total calories: 1181   Total fat: 41 g
Calories per serving: 197   Fat per serving: 7 g

──SPICED APPLE PUDDING──

1/2 pound cooking apples
1/2 cup reduced-fat margarine
1/3 cup packed brown sugar
2 eggs
1-1/2 cups self-rising flour
3/4 cup golden raisins
2 tablespoons skim milk
Nonfat yogurt and cinnamon, to serve

Preheat oven to 350F (175C). Grease a 5-cup baking dish. Peel, core and roughly chop apples. In a bowl, cream margarine and sugar together until light and fluffy.

In a separate small bowl, beat eggs. Beat into creamed mixture, a little at a time. Sift flour over mixture, then, using a metal spoon, fold in. Add apples, raisins and milk; mix together thoroughly.

Spoon mixture into greased baking dish. Bake 1 hour or until golden on top. Serve hot, with yogurt sprinkled with cinnamon.

Makes 8 servings.

Total calories: 1977
Calories per serving: 247

Total fat: 66 g
Fat per serving: 8 g

BERRY RING

1 cup blackberries
1 cup raspberries
1-1/4 cups water plus 3 tablespoons
1/4 cup sugar
5 teaspoons unflavored gelatin powder
1-1/4 cups unsweetened apple juice
Fresh berries and mint sprigs, to decorate

Into a saucepan, put blackberries and raspberries with 1-1/4 cups water and the sugar. Simmer until soft, stirring occasionally. Let cool.

In a blender or food processor, puree fruit mixture. Press through a strainer until all the juice has been extracted. Discard seeds. In a small bowl, sprinkle gelatin over the 3 tablespoons water. Set aside 2 to 3 minutes to soften. Stand bowl in a saucepan of hot water and stir until gelatin dissolves; set aside to cool slightly.

Stir gelatin and apple juice into berry juice mixture. Mix well and pour into a dampened 3-3/4-cup ring mold. Cover and refrigerate until set. To serve, turn out of mold onto a dampened serving dish. Decorate with fresh berries and mint sprigs.

Makes 4 servings.

Total calories: 508   Total fat: 1 g
Calories per serving: 127   Fat per serving: 0.3 g

MOCHA WHIP

2 ounces semisweet chocolate
1 tablespoon unflavored gelatin powder
3 tablespoons water
1/2 teaspoon instant coffee granules dissolved in 1
    tablespoon warm water
2-1/2 cups nonfat plain yogurt
2 tablespoons honey
About 1-1/2 cups sponge cake cubes (page 119)
Fresh fruit and chocolate sprinkles, to decorate

Break chocolate into pieces. In a bowl set over a pan of simmering water, melt chocolate. Let cool.

In a small bowl, sprinkle gelatin over the water. Set aside 2 to 3 minutes to soften. Stand bowl in a saucepan of hot water and stir until gelatin dissolves. Set aside to cool. In a bowl, stir together chocolate, coffee, gelatin, yogurt and honey until thoroughly combined. If, at this stage, mixture begins to set, place bowl over a saucepan of hot water for a few minutes until mixture softens again.

Layer mocha mixture and cake pieces in individual glass dishes or one large glass serving dish, beginning and ending with a mocha layer. Cover and refrigerate until set. To serve, decorate with fresh fruit and chocolate sprinkles.

Makes 6 servings.

Total calories: 1310
Calories per serving: 218

Total fat: 47 g
Fat per serving: 8 g

— SPICY DRIED FRUIT COMPOTE —

10 ounces mixed dried fruit, such as apricots, apples,
  prunes, pears, peaches, figs
1-1/4 cups unsweetened orange juice
1-1/4 cups water
1 teaspoon apple-pie spice
1/4 cup sliced almonds, toasted

Into a serving dish, place dried fruit. Combine orange juice, water and spice in a bowl.

Pour juice mixture over dried fruit; stir well to combine. Cover and refrigerate overnight.

When ready to serve, sprinkle almonds over the top of the fruit.

Makes 4 servings.

Total calories: 862   Total fat: 16 g
Calories per serving: 216   Fat per serving: 4 g

CAROB FRUIT PIZZA

1/3 cup reduced-fat margarine
1/4 cup sugar
1-1/4 cups all-purpose flour
2 tablespoons carob flour
2/3 cup light whipping cream
1/2 pound fresh fruit, such as strawberries, raspberries,
    blackberries, grapes, red currants

Preheat oven to 325F (165C). Grease a baking sheet. In a bowl, cream together margarine and sugar until light and fluffy. Sift flour and carob over mixture. Using a metal spoon, stir until mixture binds together. Knead well to form a smooth dough.

On a lightly floured surface, roll out dough to an 8-inch circle. Place dough on greased baking sheet and flute the edges of dough to make an attractive edge. Bake 30 minutes.

Remove from oven and place on a wire rack to cool. To serve, in a bowl, whip cream stiffly. Spread over chocolate crust, then top with fresh fruit. Serve immediately.

Makes 8 servings.

Total calories: 1567
Calories per serving: 196

Total fat: 79 g
Fat per serving: 10 g

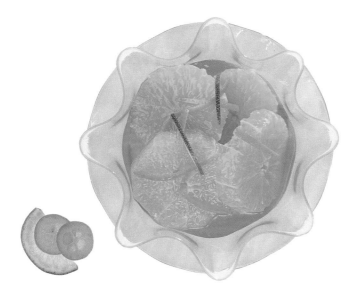

GLAZED ORANGES

4 large oranges
2-1/2 cups water
1/4 cup packed brown sugar
2 tablespoons Cointreau or other orange-flavored
  liqueur
Shredded lime peel, to decorate

Using a grater, finely grate peel from 1 orange; set aside. Peel remaining oranges, then slice thickly crosswise.

Into a saucepan, place orange slices, water, sugar and grated orange peel. Cook over medium heat until mixture comes to a boil. Reduce heat and simmer 5 minutes. Remove from heat.

Add Cointreau and stir gently. Into a serving dish, place orange slices, then leave to cool. Cover and refrigerate overnight before serving. Decorate with lime peel.

Makes 4 servings.

Total calories: 442   Total fat: 0.5 g
Calories per serving: 111   Fat per serving: 0.1 g

——TROPICAL CHOUX RING——

1/4 cup butter
2/3 cup water
1/2 cup all-purpose flour, sifted
2 eggs, beaten
1-3/4 cups cold custard (page 20)
1/2 pound pineapple, chopped
1 medium-size papaya, chopped
2 kiwifruit, chopped
1 carambola (starfruit), sliced
2 tablespoons powdered sugar

Preheat oven to 400F (205C). Grease a baking sheet. Into a saucepan, place butter and water. Simmer until butter has melted, then bring mixture to a boil.

Remove saucepan from heat. To hot mixture, add flour. Beat thoroughly until dough is smooth and forms a ball in the center of the pan. Cool slightly, then gradually add eggs, beating well after each addition, until dough is smooth and shiny. Drop tablespoons of dough onto greased baking sheet to form a ring. Bake in oven 40 minutes until puffed and browned. Remove from baking sheet carefully, transfer to a wire rack and immediately slice ring horizontally in half to release steam inside.

Leave pastry ring to cool completely. In a bowl, mix together custard sauce and prepared fruit. Spoon fruit mixture onto bottom of pastry ring. Replace top of pastry ring. To serve, sift powdered sugar over ring.

Makes 8 servings.

Total calories: 1554   Total fat: 65 g
Calories per serving: 194   Fat per serving: 8 g

Note: Place the tablespoons of dough so that they are just touching on the baking sheet.

BERRY CHEESECAKE

3 tablespoons low-fat margarine
1 cup graham cracker crumbs
1/2 pound mixed berries, such as raspberries,
   strawberries, blackberries, black and red currants
6 tablespoons water
1 tablespoon unflavored gelatin powder
1/2 cup low-fat cream cheese
3 tablespoons sugar
2/3 cup nonfat yogurt
2/3 cup light whipping cream
1 tablespoon reduced-sugar black-currant jam
Fresh mixed berries, to decorate

In a saucepan over low heat, melt margarine. Stir in cookie crumbs.

Press mixture into bottom of an 8-inch springform pan. Refrigerate 30 minutes. In a saucepan, place berries with 3 tablespoons of the water. Simmer until soft. Cool completely. In a small bowl, soften gelatin in the remaining 3 tablespoons water. Set aside 2 to 3 minutes to soften. Over a saucepan of hot water, place gelatin. Stir until dissolved. Set aside to cool slightly. In a food processor or blender, place cream cheese, sugar, yogurt, cream, cooked fruit, jam and gelatin. Blend until smooth.

Pour mixture onto cookie base. Refrigerate until set. To serve, remove from pan, place on a serving plate and decorate with mixed berries.

Makes 8 servings.

Total calories: 1542   Total fat: 79 g
Calories per serving: 193   Fat per serving: 10 g

——PLUM-CUSTARD TART——

1 pound plums
1/2 cup all-purpose flour
1/2 cup whole-wheat flour
1/4 cup low-fat margarine
1-1/4 cups skim milk
2 eggs
1/4 cup sugar
Few drops almond extract

Preheat oven to 350F (175C). Cut plums into quarters; set aside. Into a bowl, sift flours. Rub or cut in margarine until mixture resembles coarse crumbs.

Stir in enough water to make a soft dough. On a lightly floured surface, roll out dough and use to line an 8-inch quiche dish. With a fork, prick bottom of dough. Line with foil and fill with dried beans or pie weights and bake 10 minutes. Remove foil and beans. Place plums in bottom of pastry shell.

In a bowl, beat together milk, eggs, sugar and almond extract. Pour mixture over plums. Bake 45 minutes or until custard is set and golden. Serve warm or cold.

Makes 6 servings.

Total calories: 1253   Total fat: 41 g
Calories per serving: 209   Fat per serving: 7 g

Note: Almond extract is strong in flavor so use it sparingly.

GREEN FRUIT SALAD

1/2 honeydew melon
3 kiwifruit
2 green-skinned eating apples
2 pears
10 ounces seedless green grapes
1-3/4 cups white grape juice
2 tablespoons honey
Mint sprigs, to decorate

To prepare fruit, peel and remove seeds from melon. Cut flesh into chunks.

Peel kiwifruit and cut into chunks. Core apples and pears, then cut into chunks. Halve grapes, if large in size. Into a large serving dish, place fruit. In a measuring cup, mix together grape juice and honey.

Pour juice over fruit and mix gently to combine. Refrigerate before serving. Decorate with mint sprigs.

Makes 6 servings.

Total calories: 929   Total fat: 24 g
Calories per serving: 155   Fat per serving: 0.4 g

Note: Use apple juice instead of white grape juice if desired.

PEAR CRUMBLE

2 (14-oz.) cans pear halves packed in fruit juice
1 tablespoon granulated sugar
2 teaspoons ground cinnamon
1-1/4 cups whole-wheat flour
1/4 cup packed brown sugar
1/3 cup low-fat margarine

Preheat oven to 400F (205C). Into a bowl, drain pears, reserving juice. Chop pears roughly. Mix sugar with 1 teaspoon of the cinnamon and mix with pears.

In a bowl, mix together remaining cinnamon, flour and brown sugar. Rub or cut in margarine until mixture resembles coarse crumbs.

In a 5-cup baking dish, layer crumble mixture and pear mixture, pouring pear juice over fruit. Finish with a crumble layer. Bake 30 minutes or until golden on top. Serve hot or cold.

Makes 6 servings.

Total calories: 1339   Total fat: 38 g
Calories per serving: 223   Fat per serving: 6 g

——— LEMON-ORANGE CUPS ———

4 large oranges
Grated peel of 1 lemon
1/3 cup light whipping cream
1/2 cup nonfat yogurt
Julienne strips of lemon and orange peel, to decorate

With a sharp knife, cut each orange in half crosswise. Remove flesh and chop finely, then place in a bowl. Drain shells upside down on a wire rack.

Mix lemon peel and chopped orange flesh. Whip cream lightly. Mix whipped cream with yogurt. To chopped oranges, add cream mixture and stir gently to mix. Thinly slice bottom off each orange shell so they sit level on a plate.

Fill all the shells with orange mixture, then place on a serving plate. Refrigerate filled orange shells up to 30 minutes. To serve, decorate with lemon and orange peels.

Makes 6 servings.

Total calories: 519	Total fat: 21 g
Calories per serving: 65	Fat per serving: 3 g

SUMMER PUDDING

1/2 pound black currants
1/4 pound red currants
1/4 pound loganberries
1/4 pound strawberries
1/4 pound raspberries
1/4 pound blackberries
2 tablespoons honey
3 tablespoons water
8 medium-size slices whole-wheat bread

In a saucepan, place fruit, honey and water. Slowly bring mixture to a boil and cook over low heat until juicy. With a knife, cut crusts off bread, then cut bread into strips.

Line a deep 5-cup bowl with three-quarters of the bread. Place fruit in bowl and cover with remaining bread. Place a saucer with a weight on it on top of the pudding. Let cool, then refrigerate overnight.

To serve, onto a flat serving plate, turn out pudding. Serve, cut into wedges, with low-fat yogurt.

Makes 6 servings.

Total calories: 819   Total fat: 7 g
Calories per serving: 137   Fat per serving: 1 g

Note: White bread may be used in place of whole-wheat bread. Decorate the top of the pudding with red currants dipped in sugar syrup and coated with sugar, if desired.

MIXED GRAPE TARTS

3/4 cup all-purpose flour
1 teaspoon sugar
1/4 cup low-fat margarine
2/3 cup cold low-fat custard (see page 20)
3 ounces seedless green grapes
3 ounces seedless black grapes
3 tablespoons reduced-sugar apricot jam, warmed

Preheat oven to 375F (190C). Into a bowl, sift flour. Mix in sugar. Rub or cut in margarine until mixture resembles coarse crumbs. Stir in enough water to make a soft dough.

On a lightly floured surface, roll out dough. Using a 3-inch fluted cookie cutter, cut out 12 circles. Use dough circles to line 12 muffin or tart pans. With a fork, prick bottom of dough circles. Line with foil and fill with dried beans or pie weights and bake 12 to 15 minutes or until golden brown.

Cool pastry shells in pan 10 minutes, then remove from pan and place on a wire rack. Cool completely. Place a spoonful of custard sauce into each tart shell. Arrange grapes on top. Using a pastry brush, glaze with warmed apricot jam before serving.

Makes 12 tarts.

Calories per tart: 67   Fat per tart: 2 g

——— CITRUS CRUNCH TART ———

1 cup all-purpose flour
1/4 cup packed brown sugar
1/4 cup low-fat margarine
1/4 cup chopped mixed nuts
Grated peel and juice of 1 lemon
Grated peel and juice of 1 orange
4 tablespoons freshly squeezed orange juice
3 tablespoons granulated sugar
1 tablespoon cornstarch
2 eggs, separated
Lemon and lime slices, to decorate

Preheat oven to 350F (175C). Into a bowl, sift flour. Stir in brown sugar. Rub or cut in until mixture resembles coarse crumbs.

Stir in nuts and mix well. Onto bottom of a loose-bottomed 8-inch tart pan, press crumb mixture. To make filling, in a measuring cup, place fruit juices. Make up to 1-1/4 cups with water. In a saucepan, blend together granulated sugar, cornstarch and 2 tablespoons of the fruit juice. Add remaining fruit juice, grated peels and egg yolks. Heat gently, stirring constantly, or until mixture thickens. Cool 10 minutes, stirring occasionally to prevent lumps forming.

In a bowl, beat egg whites until stiff but not dry. Into fruit custard, fold egg whites. Pour custard over crust. Bake 30 to 45 minutes or until golden brown. Leave in pan to cool, then chill in the refrigerator. Decorate with lemon and lime slices. Serve cold.

Makes 6 servings.

Total calories: 1490   Total fat: 53 g
Calories per serving: 248   Fat per serving: 9 g

—— STRAWBERRY CHIFFON ——

1 (14 ounces can) strawberries in fruit juice
1 tablespoon unflavored gelatin powder
1-1/4 cups reduced-fat evaporated milk, chilled
1-1/4 cups skim milk
2/3 cup low-fat plain yogurt
1 tablespoon honey
Strawberry slices, to decorate

Drain juice from the strawberries into a bowl and make up to 1-1/4 cups with water.

Put 1/4 cup strawberry juice into a small bowl and sprinkle with gelatin. Let stand 2 to 3 minutes to soften. Place gelatin over a saucepan of hot water and stir until dissolved. Cool slightly, then pour into remaining juice and cool until starting to set. In a bowl, beat evaporated milk until thick. Gradually add half the strawberries, gelatin mix and milk and pour into a serving dish. Cover and refrigerate until set. Whisk remaining strawberries into the yogurt and honey and mix well.

Serve with yogurt sauce. Decorate with strawberry slices.

Makes 6 servings.

Total calories: 710   Total fat: 14 g
Calories per serving: 118   Fat per serving: 2 g

Note: When combining whipped milk or cheese with a gelatin mixture, it is essential that the gelatin mixture is on the point of setting, otherwise the mixture will separate out to jelly on bottom and froth on top.

—KIWI & GRAPE SPONGE TART—

2 eggs
1/4 cup sugar
1/2 cup all-purpose flour
6 ounces green grapes
2 kiwifruit
3 tablespoons reduced-sugar apricot jam

Preheat oven to 350F (175C). Grease an 8-inch raised-bottom tart pan. In a bowl, beat together eggs and sugar until mixture is very thick. Sift flour into mixture. Using a metal spoon, fold in flour.

Pour into prepared pan and level the surface. Bake 20 to 25 minutes, until light brown. Onto a wire rack, turn out cake and leave to cool. Meanwhile, halve and seed grapes. Peel and slice kiwifruit.

Arrange fruit in tart case. In a saucepan, gently heat jam with 1 tablespoon water. Cool slightly, then brush over the fruit to glaze.

Makes 6 servings.

Total calories: 827   Total fat: 18 g
Calories per serving: 138   Fat per serving: 3 g

——————BLACKBERRY MOLD——————

1/2 pound blackberries
1/4 cup sugar
4 tablespoons water
1 tablespoon unflavored gelatin powder
2-1/2 cups low-fat milk
Fresh blackberries and a mint sprig, to decorate

Into a saucepan, place blackberries and sugar with 1 tablespoon of the water. Cook gently until berries are soft. Cool, then, in a blender or food processor, puree. Cool completely.

In a small bowl, sprinkle gelatin over the remaining 3 tablespoons water. Let stand 2 to 3 minutes to soften. Place bowl in a saucepan of hot water and stir until gelatin is dissolved. Cool slightly. Mix into blackberry puree. In a bowl, mix together fruit puree and milk. Stir together well. Pour the mixture into a dampened 3-3/4-cup mold.

Cover and refrigerate until set. To serve, onto a serving plate, turn out of mold. Decorate with fresh blackberries and mint.

Makes 4 servings.

Total calories: 557	Total fat: 9 g
Calories per serving: 139	Fat per serving: 2 g

Note: The blackberry mixture must be completely cool before combining with the milk to prevent the mixture from separating.

──── PINEAPPLE FRUIT BOATS ────

1 large pineapple
1/2 pound strawberries
2 peaches
6 ounces fresh dates
1/2 cup chopped hazelnuts
Mint sprigs, to decorate

Cut pineapple in half lengthwise. Cut out core and chunks of flesh. Cut a thin slice from underneath so pineapple halves sit flat.

Halve strawberries. Peel, pit and chop peaches. Pit dates and cut into quarters. In a bowl, mix together pineapple flesh and other fruits. Pile into pineapple halves.

Sprinkle each pineapple boat with chopped hazelnuts. Decorate with mint sprigs.

Makes 6 servings.

Total calories: 1038   Total fat: 37 g
Calories per serving: 173   Fat per serving: 6 g

Note: Top pineapple boats with yogurt just before serving, if desired.

— BANANA & GINGER BRULEES —

2 cups half and half
4 egg yolks
1/3 cup sugar
2 large bananas
2 teaspoons ground ginger

Preheat oven to 300F (150C). In a saucepan, warm half and half until almost boiling. In a separate bowl, beat together egg yolks and 1/4 cup of the sugar until pale. Gradually beat cream mixture into egg mixture.

Stand 8 small ramekin dishes in a baking pan. Into pan, pour enough water to come 1/2 inch up the sides of the ramekins. Peel and slice bananas thinly. Place some banana slices in bottom of each ramekin. Sprinkle ginger over banana slices. Pour custard mixture over bananas.

Bake 1 hour or until golden on top. Cool, then refrigerate. Sprinkle remaining sugar over desserts and place under a medium grill until the sugar melts and turns brown. Cool, then refrigerate before serving.

Makes 8 servings.

Total calories: 1369   Total fat: 76 g
Calories per serving: 171   Fat per serving: 9 g

Note: Decorate with mint sprigs and fruit, if desired.

–NECTARINE MERINGUE NESTS–

3 egg whites
3/4 cup sugar
1/2 cup low-fat cream cheese
2/3 nonfat plain yogurt
3 nectarines
4 ounces black currants
2 tablespoons reduced-sugar apricot jam
1 tablespoon water

Preheat oven to 300F (150C). Line a large baking sheet with parchment paper. In a large bowl, beat egg whites until stiff but not dry. Gradually beat in sugar until mixture is stiff and glossy.

Into a pastry bag fitted with a star tip, spoon meringue. Onto the lined baking sheet, pipe meringue mixture into 6 (4-inch) rounds, leaving a gap between them. Pipe remaining meringue in stars around edge of each round to form an attractive border. Bake meringue nests 1 to 1-1/2 hours or until crisp on the outside. Cool on a wire rack. In a bowl, stir together cream cheese and yogurt, mixing well. Peel and pit nectarines and slice thinly. Remove stems from black currants. Rinse well and drain.

In a saucepan, gently heat apricot jam with water until melted. To fill each meringue nest: place some cream cheese mixture in the nest. Top with sliced nectarines and black currants, then brush with melted jam to glaze. Refrigerate until ready to serve.

Makes 6 servings.

Total calories: 1205   Total fat: 12 g
Calories per serving: 201   Fat per serving: 2 g

FILO FRUIT PASTRIES

1 Granny Smith apple
2 teaspoons lemon juice
2 kiwifruit
1 peach
1/3 cup raisins
1 teaspoon apple-pie spice
8 sheets filo pastry dough
1/4 cup low-fat margarine, melted
1 tablespoon powdered sugar
Strawberry slices, to decorate (optional)

Preheat oven to 400F (205C). To prepare filling, into a bowl, peel, core and coarsely grate apple. Sprinkle with lemon juice to prevent browning.

Peel kiwifruit, then chop roughly and add to apple. Peel, pit and chop peach roughly, then add to apple with raisins and spice. Stir well to mix. Set aside. To make each filo package, cut each filo sheet in half crosswise to make 2 (4-inch) squares (total of 16 squares). Brush 2 squares of dough lightly with melted margarine, then place one on top of the other diagonally. Place some fruit filling in the center of the dough and then fold over all the sides like a package.

Place seam-edge down on a greased baking sheet. Brush lightly with melted margarine. Repeat with remaining dough squares and filling, to make 8 packages. Bake 30 minutes or until golden and crisp. Sift powdered sugar over pastries just before serving and decorate with a few slices of strawberry, if desired. Serve hot or cold.

Makes 8 servings.

Calories per package: 135   Fat per package: 4 g

— MIXED CURRANT SENSATION —

4 ounces black currants
4 ounces red currants
4 ounces white currants
1 tablespoon honey
5 tablespoons water
1 tablespoon unflavored gelatin powder
1-3/4 cups low-fat cold custard (see page 20)
1-1/4 cups half and half
1/4 cup mixed chopped nuts

Reserve a few currants decoration. In a saucepan, place remaining currants, honey and 2 tablespoons of the water . Heat gently until just soft. Set aside to cool completely.

In a small bowl, sprinkle gelatin over remaining 3 tablespoons water. Let stand 2 to 3 minutes to soften. Place bowl in a saucepan of hot water and stir until dissolved. Cool. Into a blender or food processor, place currants and their juice, gelatin, custard and half and half. Puree until well mixed.

Into individual serving dishes, pour mixture. Cover and refrigerate until set. When ready to serve, sprinkle chopped nuts over each dessert and decorate with the reserved currants. Serve cold.

Makes 6 servings.

Total calories: 1042   Total fat: 48 g
Calories per serving: 174   Fat per serving: 8 g

Note: Desserts set more quickly if placed in a container full of cold water and ice cubes.

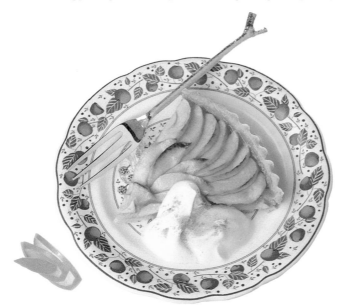

FRENCH APPLE TART

1 cup all-purpose flour
1 teaspoon sugar
1/3 cup low-fat margarine
2 pounds Granny Smith apples
2 tablespoons water
Grated peel and juice of 1 lemon
4 tablespoons reduced-sugar apricot jam
1/2 pound Golden Delicious apples

Preheat oven to 350F (175C). Into a bowl, sift flour. Mix in sugar. Rub or cut in 1/4 cup of the margarine until mixture resembles coarse crumbs. Add enough water to make a soft dough. On a lightly floured surface, roll out dough.

Use dough to line an 8-inch loose-bottomed tart pan. With a fork, prick bottom of dough all over. Bake blind 10 minutes. Peel, core and slice Granny Smith apples. Into a sauce-pan, place apple slices with remaining margarine and the 2 tablespoons water. Cover and simmer 15 minutes or until apples are soft. Add lemon peel and 3 tablespoons of the jam. Cook, stirring occasionally, 15 minutes or until thickened. Into pastry shell, spoon apple puree. Let cool. Peel, core and slice Golden Delicious apples thinly.

Arrange apple slices in an overlapping circle around edge of tart and in the center. Brush with lemon juice. Bake 30 to 40 minutes or until brown on top. Heat remaining jam and brush over tart to glaze. Serve warm or cold with yogurt sprinkled with cinnamon.

Makes 6 servings.

Total calories: 1173	Total fat: 37 g
Calories per serving: 196	Fat per serving: 6 g

——ORCHARD FRUIT SALAD——

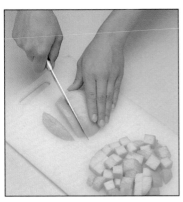

10 ounces lychees
1 medium-size mango
2 firm bananas
6 red dessert plums
2 pears
2 Gala apples
1 carambola (starfruit)
1-1/4 cups unsweetened apple juice
2/3 cup dry sherry

To prepare fruit, peel lychees, then halve and remove pits. Peel mango, then remove pit and cut flesh into chunks.

Peel and slice bananas. Halve and pit plums. Core pears and apples and cut flesh into chunks. Slice carambola thinly. Into a large serving dish, place all fruit.

In a separate bowl, mix together apple juice and sherry. Pour over the fruit and stir gently to mix. Cover and refrigerate overnight before serving.

Makes 6 servings.

Total calories: 1106   Total fat: 3 g
Calories per serving: 184   Fat per serving: 0.4 g

– PINEAPPLE & RASPBERRY LOG –

3 eggs
1/3 cup sugar
3/4 cup all-purpose flour
1 tablespoon sugar
4 tablespoons reduced-sugar raspberry jam, warmed
1 (8-oz.) can pineapple packed in fruit juice, drained
    and finely chopped
Raspberries and mint leaves, to decorate

Preheat oven to 400F (205C). Grease a 13″ ×
9″ jellyroll pan. Line with waxed paper and
grease the paper.

In a large bowl placed over a pan of hot water,
beat eggs and the 1/3 cup sugar until thick
and creamy. Remove bowl from heat and
beat until cool. Sift half the flour over
mixture and, using a large metal spoon, fold
in. Sift and fold in remaining flour together
with 1 tablespoon hot water. Pour batter into
pan and tilt to level surface. Bake 10 to 12
minutes until raised and golden. Meanwhile,
place a sheet of waxed paper over a damp dish
towel. Sprinkle paper with the 1 tablespoon
sugar.

Quickly invert cake onto the paper. Trim off
crusty edges and spread with jam. Top with
pineapple. Roll up the cake with the aid of
the paper. Place seam-side down on a wire
rack and let cool. To serve, decorate with
raspberries and mint leaves.

Makes 6 servings.

Total calories: 1159   Total fat: 25 g
Calories per serving: 193   Fat per serving: 4 g

— GOOSEBERRY-YOGURT SNOW —

12 ounces gooseberries
2 tablespoons water
1/3 cup sugar
1-3/4 cups low-fat plain yogurt
Mint sprigs, to decorate

Into a saucepan, place gooseberries and water. Cook gently over medium heat until soft, stirring occasionally.

Into gooseberries, stir sugar until dissolved. Let cool. In a blender or food processor, puree cooled gooseberries with juice and yogurt.

Pour mixture into 6 serving dishes. Cover and refrigerate until ready to serve. To serve, decorate with mint sprigs.

Makes 6 servings.

Total calories: 895   Total fat: 33 g
Calories per serving: 149   Fat per serving: 5 g

Variation: Bottled gooseberries in syrup may be used instead of fresh gooseberries; omit 1/4 cup sugar and blend gooseberries with remaining sugar and yogurt.

— BLUSHING SUMMER FRUITS —

1-1/4 cups red wine
1/3 cup sugar
Grated peel of 1 lemon
1-1/4 cups water
2 red-skinned apples
4 plums
1/2 pound strawberries
1/2 pound purple grapes
1/4 pound raspberries
Lemon slices, lemon peel and mint sprigs, to decorate

Into a saucepan, put wine, sugar, grated lemon peel and water. Bring to a boil slowly, then boil rapidly 5 minutes.

To prepare fruit, core apples and cut flesh into chunks. Halve and pit plums. Halve strawberries. Halve and seed grapes.

Into a serving dish, place all fruit. Pour the hot wine mixture over fruit. Stir gently to mix. Cool, then serve decorated with lemon slices, lemon peel and mint sprigs.

Makes 6 servings.

Total calories: 913   Total fat: 1 g
Calories per serving: 152   Fat per serving: 0.1 g

Note: If the fruits are left to soak overnight, they absorb more of the liquid, producing an even more delicious dessert!

FRESH APRICOT TART

1-1/2 cups all-purpose flour
1/3 cup low-fat margarine
10 fresh apricots
1-1/4 cups skim milk
2 eggs
3 tablespoons sugar
1 teaspoon vanilla extract

Preheat oven to 350F (175C). Into a bowl, sift flour. Rub or cut in low-fat margarine until mixture resembles bread crumbs. Add enough water to make a soft dough. On a lightly floured surface, roll out dough and use to line a loose-bottomed 8-inch tart pan.

Prick bottom of dough all over. Line with foil and fill with dried beans or pie weights and bake 10 minutes. Remove foil and beans. Peel, halve and pit apricots. Arrange over bottom of pastry shell. In a bowl, beat together milk, eggs, sugar and vanilla.

Pour mixture over apricots. Bake 30 to 45 minutes or until filling is set and golden brown. Serve warm or cold.

Makes 6 servings.

Total calories: 1496
Calories per serving: 249

Total fat: 53 g
Fat per serving: 9 g

— STRAWBERRY CHEESECAKE —

6 ounces gingersnaps
1/4 cup low-fat margarine, melted
1 tablespoon unflavored gelatin powder
3 tablespoons water
1 cup cottage cheese
3/4 cup low-fat cream cheese
1/4 cup sugar
2/3 cup light whipping cream
Grated peel of 1 lemon
1/2 pound strawberries, roughly chopped
Kiwifruit slices, to decorate

Crush gingersnaps to crumbs (about 1-1/4 cups) and mix with melted margarine.

Press crumb mixture over the bottom of a 11″ × 7″ cake pan and refrigerate until firm. In a small bowl, sprinkle gelatin over the water. Let stand 2 to 3 minutes to soften. Place bowl in a saucepan of hot water and stir until dissolved. Cool slightly. In a blender or food processor, puree together gelatin, cottage cheese, cream cheese, sugar, cream and lemon peel until smooth.

Into a bowl, pour mixture. Gently stir in strawberries until evenly distributed. Pour mixture over crumb crust and refrigerate until set. When set, cut into squares and decorate each square with kiwifruit slices.

Makes 12 servings.

Calories per square: 172   Fat per square: 9 g

—— MANDARIN DELIGHTS ——

1 (10-oz.) can mandarin orange segments packed in fruit juice
1 (1/2-oz.) package sugar-free orange-flavored gelatin
1 cup boiling water
3/4 cup unsweetened apple juice
2/3 cup low-fat plain yogurt
1/4 cup sliced almonds, toasted
Shredded orange peel

Over a bowl, drain mandarins, reserving the juice.

Dissolve flavored gelatin in 1 cup boiling water, then stir in reserved mandarin juice and apple juice. Set aside until just beginning to set. Stir mandarins into the gelatin. Pour into individual glass serving dishes. Cover and refrigerate until set.

Top each dessert with yogurt and decorate with almonds and orange peel before serving.

Makes 4 servings.

Total calories: 572   Total fat: 25 g
Calories per serving: 143   Fat per serving: 6 g

Note: Instead of mixing the mandarins into the gelatin, put them into 4 dishes, then top with gelatin. Let set, then top with yogurt.

LEMON PUDDING

1/4 cup low-fat margarine
1/2 cup sugar
Grated peel and juice of 1 lemon
2 eggs, separated
1/2 cup self-rising flour
1-1/4 cups skim milk
Grated lemon peel, to decorate

Preheat oven to 400F (205C). Grease a 3-3/4-cup baking dish. In a bowl, beat together margarine, sugar and lemon peel until light and fluffy.

Add egg yolks and mix well. Sift flour into mixture and, using a metal spoon, fold in. Add lemon juice and milk and mix thoroughly. In a separate bowl, beat egg whites until stiff but not dry. Carefully fold them into lemon mixture.

Pour mixture into baking dish. Stand dish in a shallow pan of water. Bake 45 minutes or until top is spongy to touch and browned. Serve immediately decorated with lemon peel.

Makes 6 servings.

Total calories: 1177   Total fat: 39 g
Calories per serving: 196   Fat per serving: 6 g

——— PEACH SOUFFLE OMELET ———

1 peach
2 tablespoons reduced-sugar peach or apricot jam,
  warmed
2 eggs, separated
1 teaspoon sugar
2 teaspoons powdered sugar

Peel, pit and chop peach roughly. In a small bowl, mix together peach and warmed jam; set aside. In a bowl, beat egg yolks and sugar together until creamy. In a separate bowl, beat egg whites until stiff.

Over a medium heat, heat a nonstick 7-inch omelet pan. Fold egg whites into egg yolk mixture. Pour into omelet pan. Cook over medium heat 2 or 3 minutes or until omelet is lightly browned underneath. Place pan under a preheated broiler a few minutes until top is browned. Place omelet onto a warm serving plate.

Spread with peach mixture and fold omelet over filling. Sift powdered sugar over top of omelet. Using a hot metal skewer, mark a crisscross pattern in the sugar. Serve immediately.

Makes 2 servings.

Total calories: 369   Total fat: 16 g
Calories per serving: 185   Fat per serving: 8 g

ROSY DESSERT PEARS

4 large pears
1-3/4 cups red wine
2/3 cup unsweetened orange juice
1/3 cup packed brown sugar
Grated orange peel, to decorate

Preheat oven to 400F (205C). Carefully peel pears, leaving stems intact and the fruits whole. Place in a baking dish.

In a measuring cup, mix together red wine, orange juice and sugar. Pour the liquid over pears. Cover dish and bake 1 hour or until pears are softened.

Carefully lift pears out of dish and place upright on a serving platter or individual dishes. Pour cooking liquid into a saucepan. Boil rapidly until it is reduced. Spoon liquid over the pears. Decorate with orange peel. Serve hot.

Makes 4 servings.

Total calories: 966   Total fat: 0.9 g
Calories per serving: 242   Fat per serving: 0.2 g

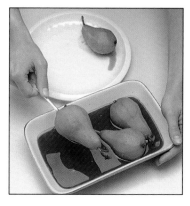

—GOOSEBERRY BROWN BETTY—

1 pound gooseberries, trimmed
2 tablespoons water
3/4 cup all-purpose flour
Pinch of salt
1 teaspoon ground cinnamon
1 cup rolled oats
1/4 cup packed brown sugar
1/4 cup low-fat margarine
2 tablespoons honey
Nonfat plain yogurt, to serve

Preheat oven to 350F (175C). In a saucepan, place gooseberries and water. Cover and simmer until fruit is just soft.

Sift flour, salt and cinnamon into a bowl. Stir in oats and sugar and mix well. Rub or cut in margarine until evenly mixed. Into a baking dish, place half the gooseberries. Dribble with 1 tablespoon of the honey and top with half the oat mixture.

Repeat these layers once more, ending with a layer of oat mixture. Bake 30 to 40 minutes or until topping is crisp and light brown. Serve hot with nonfat yogurt.

Makes 6 servings.

Total calories: 1309   Total fat: 31 g
Calories per serving: 218   Fat per serving: 5 g

──── PLUM BATTER PUDDING ────

1 cup all-purpose flour
Pinch of salt
1 egg, beaten
1-1/4 cups skim milk
9 small red plums
1/4 cup sugar

Preheat oven to 425F (220C). Grease 6 muffin cups. To make batter, into a bowl, sift flour and salt. Make a well in the center of flour and add beaten egg.

Gradually beat in milk until batter is smooth. Halve and pit plums.

Arrange 3 plum halves in bottom of each muffin cup. Sprinkle with sugar. Pour batter over fruit. Bake 20 to 25 minutes or until raised and brown. Serve immediately.

Makes 6 servings.

Total calories: 1092   Total fat: 25 g
Calories per serving: 182   Fat per serving: 4 g

Variation: Use apricots in place of plums.

—PEAR & DATE RECTANGLES—

1 pound pears
2 tablespoons water
1/3 cup sugar
1 teaspoon ground cinnamon
2/3 cup dried dates, chopped
12 sheets filo pastry dough
1/4 cup low-fat margarine, melted
2 tablespoons honey, warmed

Preheat oven to 300F (150C). Peel, core and slice pears. Into a saucepan, place pear slices and water. Cover and cook over low heat until just softened. Add sugar, cinnamon and dates, mix well and cool slightly. Trim filo pastry into sheets measuring 11″ × 7″.

Place 1 sheet of dough into the bottom of an 11″ × 7″ baking pan. Brush lightly with melted margarine. Place another sheet of dough on top, brush lightly with melted margarine and repeat with another 2 sheets of dough. Place half the fruit mixture on top. Place 4 sheets of dough on top of fruit, brushing each sheet lightly with melted margarine.

Repeat with remaining fruit mixture and dough sheets, brushing each sheet with melted margarine. Cut through the layers to make 12 rectangles. Bake about 1 hour or until golden on top. Spoon warm honey evenly over rectangles. Let stand 5 minutes.

Makes 12 servings.

Calories per slice: 147   Fat per slice: 3 g

–ORANGE SEMOLINA PUDDING–

2-1/2 cups skim milk
1 tablespoon low-fat margarine
1/4 cup Cream of Wheat cereal
1/4 cup sugar
Grated peel of 1 orange
Grated orange peel, to decorate

Preheat oven to 400F (205C). Grease a 3-3/4-cup baking dish. In a saucepan, heat together milk and margarine until almost boiling. Sprinkle with cereal.

Bring to a boil, then cook 3 minutes, stirring constantly. Remove from heat and stir in sugar and orange peel, mixing well.

Pour mixture into greased baking dish. Bake 30 minutes or until lightly browned. Serve immediately decorated with orange peel and accompanied by fresh fruit, if desired.

Makes 4 servings.

Total calories: 616   Total fat: 7 g
Calories per serving: 154   Fat per serving: 2 g

HOT LEMON SOUFFLE

3 tablespoons low-fat margarine
6 tablespoons all-purpose flour
1 cup skim milk
Grated peel and juice of 1 lemon
4 eggs, separated
1/4 cup granulated sugar
1 tablespoon powdered sugar

Preheat oven to 350F (175C). Grease a 5-cup soufle dish. In a saucepan, melt margarine. Stir in flour and cook slowly 2 minutes, stirring constantly.

Gradually stir in milk and beat until smooth. Cook, stirring, 2 minutes. Beat lemon peel and juice into sauce, together with egg yolks, one at a time. Beat in granulated sugar, mixing well. In a separate bowl, beat egg whites until stiff but not dry. Using a metal spoon, gently fold egg whites into lemon mixture.

Spoon lemon mixture into soufle dish. Bake 45 minutes or until well puffed and lightly browned. Sift powdered sugar over top and serve immediately.

Makes 6 servings.

Total calories: 1124   Total fat: 51 g
Calories per serving: 187   Fat per serving: 8 g

- APRICOT & ORANGE COMPOTE -

2-1/2 cups water
1/4 cup packed brown sugar
1 teaspoon ground cinnamon
1 teaspoon grated nutmeg
1 teaspoon ground cloves
2 tablespoons unsweetened orange juice
1 tablespoon Cointreau or other orange-flavored
    liqueur
1 (14-oz.) can apricot halves packed in fruit juice
2 large oranges, peeled and thickly sliced
Nonfat plain yogurt and ground cinnamon, to serve

In a saucepan, combine water and sugar. Cook, stirring to dissolve sugar, over low heat.

To pan, add all the spices and orange juice. Bring to a boil, reduce heat and simmer 15 minutes.

Add Cointreau, apricots and their juice and oranges and stir gently to mix. Simmer 10 to 15 minutes. Serve immediately with nonfat yogurt, sprinkled with cinnamon.

Makes 4 servings.

Total calories: 550   Total fat: 4 g
Calories per serving: 138   Fat per serving: 1 g

Note: This dessert is also delicious served chilled.

SPICY CARROT RING

1/2 cup low-fat margarine
1/2 cup packed brown sugar
2 eggs, beaten
1-1/2 cups self-rising flour
2 teaspoons apple-pie spice
Grated peel and juice of 1 lemon
1/3 cup raisins
2 cups coarsely grated carrots
1 tablespoon powdered sugar

Preheat oven to 350F (175C). Grease a 5-cup ring pan. In a bowl, cream together margarine and brown sugar until light and fluffy.

Gradually add beaten eggs, one at a time, beating well after each addition. Using a large metal spoon, fold in flour and apple-pie spice. Add lemon peel and juice, raisins and carrots. Stir gently but thoroughly to mix.

Spoon batter into greased ring pan. Bake 30 to 40 minutes or until brown. Turn out onto a wire rack. Sift powdered sugar over top. Slice and serve immediately.

Makes 8 servings.

Total calories: 2011   Total fat: 66 g
Calories per serving: 251   Fat per serving: 8 g

——— HARVEST CRUNCH ———

1/2 pound Granny Smith apples
1/2 pound pears
1/4 pound blackberries
2 tablespoons unsweetened orange juice
1/4 cup packed brown sugar
2 tablespoons low-fat margarine
2 tablespoons honey
2/3 cup rolled oats
2 cups bran flakes
Mint leaves, to decorate

Preheat oven to 350F (175C). Peel, core and slice apples and pears. Into a saucepan, place apple and pear slices with blackberries and orange juice.

Cover and simmer until just softened. Add sugar. In a separate saucepan, melt margarine and honey over low heat. Stir in oats and bran flakes and mix well. Spoon fruit mixture into 6 small ovenproof dishes.

Spoon crunch mixture over fruit. Bake 25 to 30 minutes or until crisp and browned on top. Decorate with mint leaves and serve immediately.

Makes 6 servings.

Total calories: 962   Total fat: 16 g
Calories per serving: 160   Fat per serving: 3 g

Variation: Replace the bran flakes with another crunchy cereal.

MANGO & LYCHEE TURNOVERS

1 tablespoon cornstarch
1 tablespoon granulated sugar
3 tablespoons water
3 tablespoons unsweetened orange juice
1 teaspoon lemon juice
1 teaspoon grated nutmeg
1 mango
10 lychees
8 sheets filo pastry dough
1/4 cup low-fat margarine, melted
1 tablespoon powdered sugar

Preheat oven to 400F (205C). In a saucepan, blend cornstarch, granulated sugar and water. Stir in juices and nutmeg.

Over low heat, cook, stirring, until mixture thickens. Simmer sauce 3 minutes; set aside to cool. Peel, pit and coarsely chop mango and lychees. Add fruit to cooled sauce, mixing well. To make each turnover, cut each filo sheet to make 2 (4-inch) squares (total of 16 squares). Brush 2 squares of dough lightly with melted margarine and place one on top of the other. Place some filling in the center of the dough, fold diagonally in half and press edges to seal.

Onto a greased baking sheet, place turnover. Brush lightly with melted margarine. Repeat with remaining dough and filling to make 8 turnovers. Bake 30 minutes or until golden and crisp. Sift powdered sugar over turnovers and serve warm.

Makes 8 servings.

Calories per turnover: 127   Fat per turnover: 4 g

APPLE COBBLER

12 ounces Granny Smith apples
1/4 cup packed brown sugar
1/4 cup low-fat margarine
1/4 cup granulated sugar
1 egg, beaten
1 cup self-rising flour
2 tablespoons skim milk
1/4 cup sliced almonds

Preheat oven to 350F (175C). Grease a 4-cup baking dish. Peel, core and slice apples. Arrange apple slices in bottom of greased dish.

Sprinkle brown sugar over apples. In a bowl, cream together margarine and granulated sugar until light and fluffy. Gradually add beaten egg, beating well after each addition. Using a large metal spoon, fold in flour. Stir in milk, mixing gently but thoroughly.

Spread mixture over apples. Sprinkle almonds on top. Bake 30 to 40 minutes or until apples are tender and topping is golden.

Makes 6 servings.

Total calories: 1408   Total fat: 46 g
Calories per serving: 235   Fat per serving: 8 g

BAKED BANANAS

4 medium-size bananas
2 tablespoons brandy
6 tablespoons unsweetened orange juice
2 tablespoons brown sugar
Orange twists, to decorate
Nonfat plain yogurt and orange peel, to serve

Preheat oven to 350F (175C). Peel bananas, then slice diagonally.

Into a baking dish, place banana slices. In a bowl, mix brandy, orange juice and sugar together. Pour over the bananas. Cover dish and bake 30 minutes.

Spoon bananas into a serving dish, or individual dishes. Decorate with orange twists. Serve with yogurt decorated with orange peel.

Makes 4 servings.

Total calories: 695   Total fat: 1 g
Calories per serving: 174   Fat per serving: 0.3 g

— CAROB & CHERRY PUDDING —

1 (14-oz.) can cherries in fruit juice, drained
1/2 cup low-fat margarine
1/2 cup sugar
2 eggs, beaten
1-1/2 cups self-rising flour, sifted
3 tablespoons carob flour, sifted
3 tablespoons skim milk

Grease a 5-cup heatproof bowl. Place cherries in bottom of greased bowl. In a bowl, beat together margarine and sugar until light and fluffy.

Gradually add beaten eggs, beating well after each addition. Using a metal spoon, fold in self-rising flour and carob flour. Add milk and mix gently to combine. Spoon batter over cherries and smooth surface. Cover with a double layer of greased foil and secure with string.

Place in a saucepan of gently boiling water that comes halfway up bowl. Steam 1-1/2 hours. To serve, carefully unmold onto a plate and cut into wedges.

Makes 8 servings.

Total calories: 1985   Total fat: 59 g
Calories per serving: 248   Fat per serving: 7 g

–APRICOT UPSIDE DOWN CAKE–

1 (14-oz.) can apricot halves packed in fruit juice
6 candied cherries
1/2 cup low-fat margarine
1/3 cup packed brown sugar
2 eggs, beaten
2 cups self-rising flour
5 tablespoons skim milk
Vanilla frozen yogurt, to serve

Preheat oven to 350F (175C). Grease a 9-inch cake pan. Drain apricots and halve cherries. Arrange cherries cut-side down in greased pan. Place apricot halves over cherries.

In a bowl, cream together margarine and sugar until light and fluffy. Gradually add eggs, beating well after each addition. Using a large metal spoon, fold in flour and milk to make a soft batter.

Spread mixture over apricots. Bake 45 minutes or until cake springs back when lightly pressed. Turn out cake on a wire rack, then place on a plate, bottom-side up. Serve with frozen yogurt.

Makes 8 servings.

Total calories: 2000   Total fat: 60 g
Calories per serving: 250   Fat per serving: 7 g

RHUBARB & APPLE CHARLOTTE

1-1/4 pounds fresh or frozen rhubarb
1/2 pound cooking apples
1/3 cup packed brown sugar
1/4 cup reduced-fat margarine
3 cups fresh whole-wheat bread crumbs
1/4 cup unsweetened orange juice

Preheat oven to 375F (190C). Cut fresh rhubarb into 2-inch pieces. Peel, core and slice apples.

Arrange half of the rhubarb in the bottom of a 7-cup baking dish. Cover with half of the apple slices. Sprinkle with half of the sugar and dot with some of the margarine. Cover with half of the bread crumbs. Repeat layers, ending with a layer of bread crumbs.

Pour orange juice over crumbs. Bake 40 minutes or until fruit is tender and top is browned.

Makes 6 servings.

Total calories: 1259   Total fat: 27 g
Calories per serving: 210   Fat per serving: 4 g

Note: Use fresh white bread crumbs in place of whole-wheat bread crumbs, if you like.

— BLACKBERRY-APPLE COBBLER —

1 pound cooking apples
8 ounces blackberries
2 tablespoons water
1/3 cup sugar
2 cups self-rising flour
Pinch of salt
2 teaspoons ground mixed spice
3 tablespoons reduced-fat margarine
2/3 cup skim milk

Preheat oven to 425F (220C). Peel, core and slice apples and place in a saucepan with blackberries and water. Cover and simmer until just soft, stirring occasionally. Mix in 1/4 cup sugar; pour into a 7-cup baking dish.

Sift flour into a bowl with salt and mixed spice. Rub or cut in margarine until mixture resembles coarse crumbs, then stir in remaining sugar. Add enough milk to make a soft dough. Roll out dough on a lightly floured surface and cut out 12 (2-inch) rounds.

Place rounds around edge of dish on top of fruit, overlapping them slightly. Brush rounds with a little milk. Bake 15 to 20 minutes or until browned.

Makes 6 servings.

Total calories: 1503   Total fat: 22 g
Calories per serving: 251   Fat per serving: 4 g

—— RUM & RAISIN CREPES ——

CREPES:
1/2 cup whole-wheat flour
1/2 cup all-purpose flour
Pinch of salt
1 egg
1-1/4 cups skim milk
2 teaspoons sunflower oil
SAUCE:
1 tablespoon cornstarch
1/4 cup packed brown sugar
1-1/2 cups orange juice
1/3 cup raisins
3 tablespoons white rum

Into a large bowl, sift flours and salt. Make a well in the center.

Beat together egg and milk, then pour into the well. Using a wooden spoon, gradually mix flour into liquid, keeping batter smooth. Beat well. Leave to stand at least 30 minutes. Meanwhile, make sauce. In a saucepan, blend cornstarch and sugar with orange juice. Stir in raisins. Cook over low heat, stirring constantly, until sauce thickens. Add rum and simmer 3 minutes. Keep warm while making crepes. Heat a 7-inch heavy bottomed skillet and grease lightly with oil.

Pour in just enough batter to cover the bottom of pan (scant 1/4 cup). Cook over medium heat 1 to 2 minutes or until underside is lightly browned. Turn or toss crepe and cook other side. Turn out and keep warm while cooking remaining crepes. Serve crepes with raisin sauce poured over them.

Makes 8 servings.

Calories per crepe: 161   Fat per crepe: 3 g

–RASPBERRY & APPLE STRUDEL–

1/2 pound cooking apples, peeled, cored and sliced
1/2 pound raspberries
2 tablespoons water
1/4 cup granulated sugar
1/2 pound chopped mixed nuts
1 teaspoon ground cinnamon
8 sheets filo pastry dough
1/4 cup reduced-fat margarine, melted
1 tablespoon powdered sugar

Preheat oven to 375F (190C). Grease a baking sheet. Into a saucepan, put apples, raspberries and water. Cover and simmer until just soft. Stir in granulated sugar and cool. Stir in nuts and cinnamon.

Place one sheet of pastry dough on a sheet of parchment paper. Brush dough lightly with margarine. Place another sheet of dough on top, then layer remaining sheets of dough on top of one another, brushing each one lightly with margarine. Spoon fruit mixture over dough leaving a 1-inch border uncovered all around edge. Fold these edges over fruit mixture.

With a long side toward you, using parchment paper, roll up strudel. Carefully place it on greased baking sheet, seam-side down. Brush lightly with margarine. Bake about 40 minutes or until browned. Sift with powdered sugar.

Makes 8 servings.

Total calories: 1409   Total fat: 57 g
Calories per serving: 176   Fat per serving: 7 g

CARROT PUDDING

1/2 cup reduced-fat margarine
1/3 cup packed brown sugar
2 eggs, beaten
1-1/2 cups self-rising flour, sifted
1 cup coarsely grated carrots
1/3 cup golden raisins
3 tablespoons skim milk
Low-fat custard sauce, to serve

Grease a deep 5-cup heatproof bowl. In a bowl, cream together margarine and sugar until light and fluffy. Gradually add beaten eggs, beating well after each addition.

Using a metal spoon, stir in flour, carrots, raisins and milk, mixing gently to combine. Spoon batter into greased bowl. Level surface.

Cover with a double layer of parchment paper and secure with string. Place bowl in a saucepan of gently boiling water that comes halfway up bowl. Steam 1-1/2 hours. To serve, turn out onto a plate. Serve with low-fat custard sauce.

Serves 8.

Total calories: 1810   Total fat: 65 g
Calories per serving: 226   Fat per serving: 8 g

BREAD PUDDING

6 thin slices whole-wheat bread, crusts removed
2 tablespoons reduced-fat margarine
2 tablespoons reduced-sugar strawberry jam
1/3 cup golden raisins
2 tablespoons brown sugar
2 eggs
2-1/2 cups skim milk
Nonfat yogurt and cinnamon, to serve

Grease a rectangular 1-1/2-quart baking dish. Spread one side of the bread slices with margarine. Spread the other side with jam.

Using a knife, cut bread into small triangles. Place half the bread shapes in a greased baking dish. Sprinkle with raisins and half of the sugar. Arrange remaining bread, margarine-side up, down center of dish and sprinkle with remaining sugar.

In a bowl, beat together eggs and milk. Strain this mixture into dish over bread. Let stand 30 minutes, so bread absorbs some of the liquid. Meanwhile, preheat oven to 325F (165C). Bake about 1 hour or until set and browned. Serve warm or hot with yogurt sprinkled with cinnamon.

Makes 6 servings.

Total calories: 1112
Calories per serving: 185

Total fat: 31 g
Fat per serving: 5 g

── STRAWBERRY-YOGURT ICE ──

1 pound strawberries
1/2 cup sugar
1-1/4 cups low-fat strawberry-flavored yogurt
1 cup low-fat cream cheese
Mint sprigs and fresh strawberries, to decorate

In a blender or food processor, puree straw-berries until smooth.

To food processor or blender, add sugar, yogurt and cream cheese. Blend until thoroughly mixed. Pour mixture into a chilled, shallow plastic container. Cover and freeze 1-1/2 to 2 hours or until mixture is mushy in consistency. Turn out mixture into a chilled bowl. Beat with a fork or electric mixer until smooth.

Return mixture to container, cover and freeze until firm. Transfer to refrigerator 30 minutes before serving to soften. Serve in scoops, decorated with mint sprigs and fresh strawberries.

Makes 6 servings.

Total calories: 1013   Total fat: 3 g
Calories per serving: 169   Fat per serving: 0.5 g

KIWIFRUIT ICE

6 kiwifruit
1 tablespoon lemon juice
1/2 cup sugar
1-1/4 cups water
4 ripe passion fruit
Cookies, to serve (optional)

Slice kiwifruit into a blender or food processor; add lemon juice. Blend until smooth; set aside.

Into a saucepan, put sugar and water. Cook, stirring, until sugar dissolves, then boil 10 minutes. Stir in kiwifruit puree and set aside to cool. Place cooled mixture into a chilled, shallow plastic container. Cover and freeze 1-1/2 to 2 hours or until the mixture is mushy in consistency. Turn out mixture into a chilled bowl.

Cut each passion fruit in half and scoop out flesh. Add to frozen mixture. Beat with a fork or electric mixer until smooth. Return mixture to container, cover and freeze until firm. Transfer to the refrigerator about 15 minutes before serving to soften. Serve in scoops in individual dishes or glasses, accompanied by cookies, if desired.

Makes 6 servings.

Total calories: 681	Total fat: 2 g
Calories per serving: 114	Fat per serving: 0.3 g

COFFEE BOMBE

1-1/4 cups half and half
1-1/4 cups plain yogurt
2 teaspoons instant coffee powder
1 tablespoon hot water
1/2 cup powdered sugar, sifted

Lightly butter a 4-cup bombe mold or deep bowl. In a large bowl, mix half and half and yogurt together.

Dissolve coffee powder in water. Using a large metal spoon, stir coffee mixture and sugar into yogurt mixture. Mix gently but thoroughly. Pour mixture into greased bombe mold. Cover and freeze until firm.

Transfer bombe to the refrigerator 45 minutes before serving to soften slightly. Unmold onto a serving dish.

Makes 8 servings.

Total calories: 805   Total fat: 43 g
Calories per serving: 101   Fat per serving: 5 g

Note: Decorate with sliced almonds, if desired, but this will increase the calorie count.

—— MIXED BERRY SHERBET ——

1/4 pound raspberries
1/4 pound black currants
1/4 pound strawberries
1/2 cup sugar
2 tablespoons water
2-1/2 cups skim milk
1-1/4 cups plain yogurt
Fresh berries, to decorate

Into a saucepan, place fruit, sugar and water. Cover and, over low heat, cook gently until soft. Leave to cool completely.

Into a blender or food processor, put cooked fruit, milk and yogurt. Blend until smooth. Pour mixture into a chilled, shallow plastic container. Cover and freeze 1-1/2 to 2 hours or until the mixture is mushy in consistency.

Turn out mixture into a chilled bowl. Beat with a fork or electric beater until smooth. Return mixture to container, cover and freeze until firm. Transfer to the refrigerator 30 minutes before serving to soften. Serve in scoops, decorated with mixed berries.

Makes 6 servings.

Total calories: 1274   Total fat: 51 g
Calories per serving: 212   Fat per serving: 8 g

MANDARIN CRUSH

1 (10-oz.) can mandarin oranges packed in fruit juice
1/4 cup sugar
1-3/4 cups low-fat plain yogurt
Fresh orange wedges and peel, to decorate

Into a blender or food processor, put mandarins and juice, sugar and yogurt. Blend until smooth and well mixed.

Pour mandarin-and-yogurt mixture into a chilled, shallow plastic container. Cover and freeze 1-1/2 to 2 hours or until the mixture is mushy in consistency. Into a chilled bowl, turn out mixture. Whisk or beat with an electric mixer until the mixture is smooth.

Return mixture to container, cover and freeze until firm. Transfer to the refrigerator 30 minutes before serving to soften. Serve in scoops, decorated with orange wedges and peel.

Makes 4 servings.

Total calories: 504   Total fat: 5 g
Calories per serving: 126   Fat per serving: 1 g

──CAROB-RAISIN ICE CREAM──

2 cups skim milk
3 tablespoons sugar
1 tablespoon cornstarch
Pinch of salt
3 egg yolks
4 ounces unsweetened carob chips
2/3 cup raisins
1/2 cup low-fat plain yogurt
Cookies, to serve (optional)

Into a saucepan, pour milk. Heat gently until almost boiling. In a bowl, blend sugar, corn-starch, salt and egg yolks together. Gradually pour hot milk over mixture, stirring constantly.

Return mixture to saucepan and heat gently until mixture thickens, stirring constantly. Bring to a boil, then boil 1 minute, stirring. In a small bowl set over a pan of simmering water, melt carob chips. Add melted carob and raisins to custard, mixing well. Let cool. Gradually blend yogurt into custard, mixing well. Pour mixture into a chilled, shallow plastic container. Cover and freeze 1-1/2 to 2 hours or until the mixture is mushy in consistency. Into a chilled bowl, turn out mixture. Beat with a fork or electric mixer until smooth.

Return mixture to container, cover and freeze 1 hour. Beat mixture as before and return to container. Cover and freeze until firm. Transfer to the refrigerator 30 minutes before serving to soften. Serve in individual glass dishes with cookies, if desired.

Makes 6 servings.

Total calories: 1461   Total fat: 47 g
Calories per serving: 243   Fat per serving: 8 g

PLUM ICE

10 ounces plums, such as damsons
1/4 cup sugar
2 tablespoons water
1-1/4 cups reduced-fat evaporated milk, chilled
1-1/4 cups low-fat plain yogurt
Mint sprigs, to decorate

Into a saucepan, place plums, sugar and water. Cover and cook over low heat until just soft. Cool, then remove seeds. In a blender or food processor, place plums. Blend until smooth. Cool completely.

In a large bowl, beat evaporated milk until thick. Fold in yogurt and plum puree, mixing gently but thoroughly. Pour mixture into a chilled, shallow plastic container. Cover and freeze 1-1/2 to 2 hours or until the mixture is mushy in consistency. Turn out mixture into a chilled bowl. Whisk or beat with an electric mixer until smooth.

Return mixture to container, cover and freeze 1 hour. Beat mixture as before and return to container. Cover and freeze until firm. Transfer to the refrigerator 30 minutes before serving to soften. Serve in scoops, decorated with mint sprigs.

Makes 6 servings.

Total calories: 795   Total fat: 12 g
Calories per serving: 132   Fat per serving: 2 g

——BROWN BREAD ICE CREAM——

2-1/2 cups fresh whole-wheat bread crumbs
1/3 cup packed brown sugar
1-3/4 cups low-fat cold custard sauce (page 20)
2/3 cup plain yogurt
Grated peel and juice of 1 lemon
2 tablespoons powdered sugar, sifted
Lemon peel, to decorate
Cookies, to serve (optional)

Preheat oven to 400F (205C). Place bread crumbs on a greased baking sheet and sprinkle brown sugar over the top. Bake in oven 10 minutes, stirring occasionally, until sugar caramelizes and crumbs are golden.

Set aside crumbs to cool completely. Using a fork, break-up cooled crumbs. In a bowl, mix together custard sauce, yogurt, lemon peel and juice and powdered sugar. Pour into a chilled, shallow plastic container. Cover and freeze 1-1/2 to 2 hours or until mixture is mushy in consistency.

Turn out mixture into a chilled bowl. Beat with a fork or electric mixer until smooth. Fold in bread crumbs. Return mixture to container, cover and freeze until firm. Transfer to the refrigerator 45 minutes before serving to soften. Serve in scoops, decorated with lemon peel and accompanied by cookies, if desired.

Makes 6 servings.

Total calories: 1374   Total fat: 20 g
Calories per serving: 229   Fat per serving: 3 g

— BLACK CURRANT TERRINE —

2 cups skim milk
5 tablespoons granulated sugar
1 tablespoon cornstarch
Pinch of salt
3 egg yolks
1-2/3 cups plain yogurt
1 teaspoon vanilla extract
1/2 pound fresh black currants
2 tablespoons water
1/2 cup powdered sugar
Mint sprigs, to decorate

Into a saucepan, pour milk. Cook over low heat until almost boiling. In a bowl, blend together sugar, cornstarch, salt and egg yolks.

Gradually pour in milk, whisking constantly. Return mixture to saucepan and cook over low heat until thick, stirring. Bring to a boil, then boil 1 minute, stirring. Pour into a bowl and cool. In a bowl, using a metal spoon, fold yogurt and vanilla into custard. Pour mixture into a 9" × 5" loaf pan. Cover and freeze 1-1/2 to 2 hours or until mushy. Turn out into a chilled bowl. Beat with a fork or electric mixer until smooth. Return to loaf pan and freeze until firm. Meanwhile, into a saucepan, place black currants and water. Cover and cook until just soft; cool.

In a blender or food processor, blend black currants and powdered sugar until smooth; strain, if desired. Transfer terrine to the refrigerator 30 minutes before serving to soften. Turn out terrine onto a serving plate. Pour black currant sauce over top. Cut into slices. Spoon sauce over each serving. Decorate with mint sprigs.

Makes 8 servings.

Total calories: 1767   Total fat: 78 g
Calories per serving: 221   Fat per serving: 10 g

LEMON & LIME FROZEN YOGURT

2-1/2 cups low-fat plain yogurt
1/3 cup sugar
Grated peel and juice of 1 lemon
Grated peel and juice of 1 lime
Lime slices and shredded lemon and lime peel,
  to decorate

In a bowl, beat yogurt and sugar together
until sugar dissolves.

Add grated fruit peels and juices; mix
together well. Pour into a chilled, shallow
plastic container. Cover and freeze 1-1/2 to 2
hours or until mushy in consistency. Turn out
mixture into a chilled bowl. Whisk or beat
with an electric mixer until smooth. Return
mixture to container, cover and freeze until
firm.

Transfer to the refrigerator 30 minutes before
serving to soften. Serve in scoops, decorated
with lime slices and strips of lime and lemon
peel.

Makes 4 servings.

Total calories: 645   Total fat: 4 g
Calories per serving: 161   Fat per serving: 1 g

Variation: For a slightly less tangy flavor,
substitute grated peel and juice of 1 orange for
the lime.

—BANANA & RUM ICE CREAM—

1 pound bananas
1-1/4 cups milk
1-1/4 cups nonfat plain yogurt
3 tablespoons rum
5 tablespoons honey
1/4 cup chopped walnuts
Cookies, to serve (optional)

Peel bananas. Into a large bowl, put bananas, then mash with a fork.

Add milk, yogurt, rum, honey and walnuts and beat well to mix. Pour mixture into a chilled, shallow plastic container. Cover and freeze 1-1/2 to 2 hours or until the mixture is mushy in consistency. Into a chilled bowl, turn out mixture. Beat with a fork or whisk until smooth.

Return mixture to container, cover and freeze until firm. Transfer to the refrigerator 30 minutes before serving to soften. Serve in scoops in individual glasses with cookies, if desired.

Makes 6 servings.

Total calories: 1371   Total fat: 32 g
Calories per serving: 228   Fat per serving: 5 g

FRESH FRUIT SAVARIN

1 (1/4-oz.) package active dry yeast
1 teaspoon sugar
6 tablespoons warm skim milk (110F, 45C)
2 cups bread flour
1/2 teaspoon salt
2 tablespoons sugar
4 eggs, beaten
1/2 cup reduced-fat margarine
1/4 cup honey
2 tablespoons each water and brandy
12 ounces prepared fresh fruit, such as kiwifruit,
   strawberries, peaches, raspberries, bananas
1/4 cup sliced almonds, toasted
Mint leaves, to decorate

Grease a 5-cup savarin or ring mold. In a large bowl, blend together yeast, sugar, milk and 1/2 cup of the flour. Let stand in a warm place until frothy, about 15 minutes. Add remaining flour, salt, sugar, eggs and margarine to the yeast mixture . Beat well 5 minutes. Pour into mold, cover with a clean dish towel and let rise in a warm place 15 minutes. Preheat oven to 400F (205C). Bake 30 minutes or until browned.

Unmold savarin onto a plate. Into a saucepan, place honey and water. Heat until hot. Add brandy. Spoon over savarin while still hot. Cool. Transfer to a serving plate and arrange fruit into center of savarin. Sprinkle with almonds and decorate with mint leaves.

Makes 10 servings.

Total calories: 2326   Total fat: 97 g
Calories per serving: 233   Fat per serving: 10 g

CREME CARAMELS

Generous 1/2 cup sugar
2/3 cup water
4 eggs
1/2 cups skim milk
Few drops vanilla extract

Preheat oven to 325F (165C). Into a saucepan, put 1/3 cup sugar and water. Cook, stirring, until sugar dissolves, then bring mixture to a boil and boil, without stirring, until it caramelizes to a golden color.

Pour caramel into 6 warmed ramekin dishes, making sure the bottoms are completely covered. In a bowl, lightly beat together eggs and remaining sugar. In a saucepan, warm milk. Pour milk over eggs and sugar. Beat in vanilla, then strain over cooled caramel.

Stand ramekins in a shallow roasting pan of water. Bake about 45 minutes or until set. Leave in the dishes until cold, then turn out onto serving plates. Refrigerate until ready to serve.

Makes 6 servings.

Total calories: 1135   Total fat: 33 g
Calories per serving: 189   Fat per serving: 5 g

──HOT CHOCOLATE SOUFFLE──

3 ounces semisweet chocolate
2/3 cup skim milk
1/4 cup granulated sugar
1/2 cup all-purpose flour
2 tablespoons water
1 tablespoon reduced-fat margarine, cut into pieces
4 eggs, separated
1 tablespoon powdered sugar

Preheat oven to 400F (205C). Grease a 5-cup soufflé dish. In a small bowl set over a pan of simmering water, melt chocolate.

Into another saucepan, put milk and granulated sugar. Heat gently until almost boiling. Add chocolate and mix well. In a bowl, blend flour and water. Gradually add chocolate mixture, blending well. Return to saucepan, bring to a boil over low heat, stirring constantly, and cook 3 minutes. Add margarine, mix well and cool.

Stir in egg yolks. In a bowl, beat egg whites until stiff but not dry. Using a metal spoon, fold egg whites into chocolate mixture. Pour into soufflé dish. Bake about 35 minutes or until puffed and firm to touch. Sift powdered sugar over soufflé and serve immediately.

Makes 6 servings.

Total calories: 1461
Calories per serving: 244

Total fat: 64 g
Fat per serving: 11 g

— PEACH MELBA CHEESECAKE —

1/4 cup reduced-fat margarine
3 tablespoons honey
3 cups corn flakes
1/4 cup mixed chopped nuts
1 (14-oz.) can peach slices packed in fruit juice
1 tablespoon unflavored gelatin powder
6 ounces raspberries
1-1/4 cups low-fat cream cheese
1/4 cup sugar
2/3 cup nonfat yogurt
2/3 cup half and half
Fresh peach slices and raspberries, to decorate

In a saucepan, over low heat, melt margarine and honey.

Stir in corn flakes and nuts, mixing well. Press mixture over bottom of an 8-inch loose-bottomed tart pan. Refrigerate 30 minutes. Over a small bowl, drain peaches. Sprinkle gelatin over peach juice and set aside 2 to 3 minutes to soften. Stand bowl in a saucepan of hot water and stir until gelatin dissolves. Cool slightly. In a blender or food processor, place peaches, raspberries, cream cheese, sugar, yogurt, half and half and gelatin. Blend until smooth and well mixed.

Pour over chilled crust and level surface. Cover and refrigerate until set. To serve, remove cheesecake from pan and place on a serving plate. Decorate with fresh peach slices and raspberries just before serving.

Makes 8 servings.

Total calories: 1944   Total fat: 57 g
Calories per serving: 243   Fat per serving: 7 g

FESTIVAL GATEAU

3 egg whites
3/4 cup sugar
1/2 teaspoon vanilla extract
1/2 teaspoon white-wine vinegar
1 teaspoon cornstarch
1 cup light whipping cream
2 kiwifruit
4 ounces strawberries
4 ounces raspberries

Preheat oven to 225F (105C). Draw 2 (8-inch) circles on parchment paper, place paper, marked-sides down, on 2 baking sheets. In a large bowl, beat egg whites until stiff.

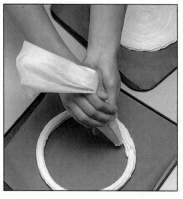

Beat in half of the sugar, then using a metal spoon, gently fold in remaining sugar, vanilla, vinegar and cornstarch. Spread or pipe meringue over circles on parchment on baking sheets. Bake 1 to 1-1/2 hours or until dry. Transfer to a wire rack to cool. Meanwhile, to prepare filling, in a bowl, beat cream until thick. Peel kiwifruit and slice. Halve strawberries. In a separate bowl, gently mix fruit together. To assemble gateau, place one meringue circle, flat-side down, on a serving plate.

Spread it with most of the cream, reserving a little for piping. Place most of the fruit on top of the cream, reserving some pieces for decoration. Top with second meringue circle, flat-side down. Pipe remaining cream decoratively on top of the gateau and decorate with remaining pieces of fruit. Serve immediately.

Makes 8 servings.

Total calories: 1480   Total fat: 73 g
Calories per serving: 185   Fat per serving: 9 g

— STRAWBERRY PROFITEROLES —

1/2 cup all-purpose flour
1/4 cup reduced-fat margarine
2/3 cup water
2 eggs, beaten
2/3 cup light whipping cream
8 ounces strawberries
2 tablespoons powdered sugar

Preheat oven to 400F (205C). Line 2 baking sheets with parchment paper. Sift flour onto a plate. Place margarine and 2/3 cup water into a saucepan. Cook over low heat until margarine has melted, then bring to a boil. Remove from heat, add flour and beat until mixture leaves the sides of the pan.

Gradually beat in eggs until mixture is smooth and shiny. Spoon mixture into a pastry bag fitted with a medium-size plain tip. Pipe walnut-size balls onto prepared baking sheets. Bake 20 to 25 minutes until brown and crisp. Make a slit in side of each profiterole to let steam escape. Cool on a wire rack. In a bowl, beat cream until stiff. Spoon into a pastry bag fitted with a medium-size plain tip. Pipe some cream into each profiterole.

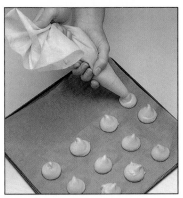

Halve strawberries and place some strawberries into each profiterole. Arrange profiteroles on a serving dish. Sift powdered sugar over profiteroles. Serve immediately.

Makes 6 servings.

Total calories: 962   Total fat: 75 g
Calories per serving: 120   Fat per serving: 9 g

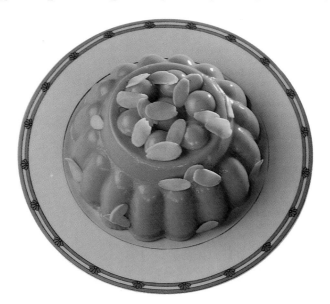

COFFEE-ALMOND BLANCMANGE

1/4 cup cornstarch
1/4 cup sugar
2-1/2 cups skim milk
2 teaspoons instant coffee powder
1 tablespoon warm water
1 tablespoon reduced-fat margarine
1/4 cup sliced almonds, toasted

In a bowl, blend cornstarch and sugar with 2 tablespoons of the milk. In a saucepan, place remaining milk. Heat until almost boiling.

Pour hot milk over cornstarch mixture, stirring well. Return mixture to saucepan and cook over low heat until mixture boils and thickens, stirring constantly. In a small bowl, blend coffee powder with 1 tablespoon warm water. Add to custard with reduced-fat margarine and cook 3 minutes longer.

Pour mixture into a 3-3/4-cup dampened mold; set aside to cool slightly. Cover and refrigerate until set. To serve, turn out mold onto a serving plate. Sprinkle with almonds.

Makes 4 servings.

Total calories: 823   Total fat: 21 g
Calories per serving: 206   Fat per serving: 5 g

— BANANA & PINEAPPLE TRIFLE —

3 tablespoons reduced-sugar peach or apricot jam
6 slices sponge cake (page 119)
1 (8-oz.) can pineapple chunks packed in fruit juice
2 tablespoons brandy
2 bananas
1/2 ounce package sugar-free pineapple gelatin
1-1/4 cups low-fat cold custard (page 20)
1-1/4 cups nonfat yogurt
Glace pineapple and angelica, to decorate

Spread jam on cake slices, then cut into fingers. Place in bottom of a glass serving dish. Drain pineapple cubes, reserving juice.

Mix together pineapple juice and brandy and pour over cake fingers. Peel and slice bananas. Arrange pineapple cubes and banana slices over cake slices. Dissolve gelatin mixture in 1 cup boiling water, then add 1 cup cold water. Let cool.

Pour gelatin mixture over fruit. Cover and refrigerate until set. In a bowl, mix together cold custard and yogurt. Spread over gelatin, decorate with crystallized pineapple and angelica and serve.

Makes 6 servings.

Total calories: 1365   Total fat: 8 g
Calories per serving: 228   Fat per serving: 1 g

——— TROPICAL MELON CUPS ———

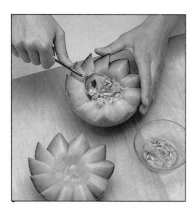

1 large honeydew melon
8 ounces pineapple
1 papaya
10 fresh dates
2 kiwifruit
1-1/4 cups unsweetened tropical fruit juice
1-1/4 cups dry sherry

Cut melon in half crosswise in a zigzag pattern and remove seeds. Using a melon baller, hollow out flesh. Into a large bowl, place melon balls.

Prepare remaining fruit. Skin and core pineapple, then chop flesh into small cubes. Peel, seed and chop papaya coarsely. Halve and pit dates. Peel and slice kiwifruit. Mix fruit with melon balls. Pile fruit into melon halves, serving any leftover fruit separately.

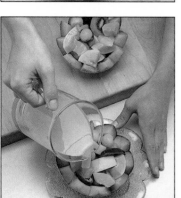

In a pitcher, mix together fruit juice and sherry. Pour over fruit. Cover and refrigerate until ready to serve.

Makes 6 servings.

Total calories: 1137   Total fat: 3 g
Calories per serving: 189   Fat per serving: 0.4 g

—BLACK CURRANT MOUSSE—

1/2 pound fresh black currants
5 tablespoons water
2 cups skim milk
1/3 cup sugar
1 tablespoon cornstarch
Pinch of salt
3 egg yolks
5 teaspoons unflavored gelatin powder
1-1/4 cups half and half
Black currants, to decorate

Into a saucepan, put black currants and 2 tablespoons of the water. Simmer, stirring occasionally, until just softened. Cool, then in a blender, puree until smooth.

In another saucepan, blend together milk, sugar, cornstarch, salt and egg yolks. Cook over low heat, stirring constantly, until mixture thickens. Bring to a boil and boil 1 minute. In a small bowl, sprinkle gelatin over remaining 3 tablespoons water. Set aside 2 to 3 minutes to soften. Stand bowl in a saucepan of hot water and stir until gelatin dissolves. Cool slightly. Stir gelatin and black currant puree into custard mixture.

In a bowl, mix custard mixture and half and half together. Pour mixture into a dampened 5-cup mold and refrigerate until set. To serve, turn out onto a serving plate. Decorate with currants.

Makes 6 servings.

Total calories: 1254   Total fat: 47 g
Calories per serving: 209   Fat per serving: 8 g

CAROB-HAZELNUT CHEESECAKE

3/4 cup whole-wheat flour
1/4 cup carob flour
1/4 cup reduced-fat margarine
4 ounces unsweetened carob chips
1 cup low-fat cream cheese
2/3 cup nonfat yogurt
1/4 cup honey
1/4 cup chopped hazelnuts
2 eggs, separated
1 tablespoon powdered sugar

Preheat oven to 350F (175C). Into a bowl, sift flours. Rub or cut in margarine until mixture resembles bread crumbs. Stir in enough water to make a soft dough.

On a lightly floured surface, roll out dough. Use to line bottom of an 8-inch loose-bottomed tart pan. In a small bowl set over a saucepan of simmering water, melt carob chips. Set aside to cool. In a large bowl, beat melted carob, cream cheese, yogurt, honey, nuts and egg yolks together until well mixed. In another bowl, beat egg whites until stiff. Using a metal spoon, gently fold beaten egg whites into carob mixture.

Pour mixture over dough. Bake 45 minutes or until firm to touch. Transfer to a wire rack to cool, then refrigerate until chilled. To serve, remove cheesecake from pan and sift powdered sugar over cheesecake.

Makes 8 servings.

Total calories: 1753   Total fat: 74 g
Calories per serving: 219   Fat per serving: 9 g

Variation: Serve with yogurt and a sprinkling of nuts, if wished.

— TROPICAL FRUIT CLUSTERS —

1 mango
1 orange
1 banana
1 apple
1/3 cup packed brown sugar
8 sheets filo pastry dough
1/4 cup reduced-fat margarine, melted
1 tablespoon powdered sugar

Preheat oven to 400F (205C). Grease a baking sheet. Prepare filling: Peel, pit and chop mango and put into a bowl. Segment orange, squeezing out any juice, then add to mango. Peel and slice banana. Peel, core and coarsely grate apple.

Add banana, apple and brown sugar to mango mixture and mix well; set aside. To make each fruit cluster: cut each filo pastry dough sheet in half crosswise to make 2 (4-inch) squares (total of 16 squares). Brush 2 squares of dough lightly with melted margarine and place one diagonally on top of the other. Place some filling in center of dough.

Gather up dough over filling and tie up with string. Place on greased baking sheet. Brush lightly with melted margarine. Repeat with remaining dough squares and filling to make 8 clusters. Bake 30 minutes or until golden and crisp. Carefully remove string from each cluster before serving. Sift powdered sugar over pastries just before serving. Serve hot or cold.

Makes 8 servings.

Calories per serving: 162   Fat per serving: 3.4 g

– WHITE WINE & GRAPE MOLDS –

5 teaspoons unflavored gelatin powder
3 tablespoons water
1/4 cup sugar
1-1/4 cups unsweetened apple juice
1-1/4 cups medium-dry white wine
10 ounces seedless green grapes, cut into halves
Mint sprigs, to decorate

In a small bowl, sprinkle gelatin over 3 tablespoons water. Set aside 2 to 3 minutes to soften. Stand bowl in a saucepan of hot water and stir until gelatin dissolves. Cool slightly.

In another saucepan, put sugar and apple juice. Cook, stirring, until sugar dissolves. Add wine and gelatin to apple juice and mix well; set aside until just beginning to set. Stir grapes into the gelatin mixture, then pour into 4 dampened 1-1/4-cup molds. Cover and refrigerate until set.

To serve, turn out molds onto serving plates. Decorate with mint sprigs.

Makes 4 servings.

Total calories: 812   Total fat: 0.6 g
Calories per serving: 203   Fat per serving: 0.1 g

FRESH FRUIT PLATTER

4 teaspoons reduced-fat margarine
2 tablespoons all-purpose flour
1-1/4 cups low-fat milk
5 teaspoons sugar
1 mango, pureed
1 melon
4 kiwifruit
2 peaches
4 red plums
2 bananas
4 ounces raspberries
6 ounces strawberries
8 ounces green grapes, in small bunches

To make mango sauce, in a saucepan, melt margarine. Remove from heat. Stir in flour, then gradually stir in milk, blending well. Bring slowly to a boil, stirring constantly. Cook, stirring, until mixture thickens. Simmer 3 minutes. Remove from heat and add sugar and mango puree, mixing well. Serve mango sauce hot or cold with fruit. To prepare fruit, peel melon, remove seeds and cut into small slices. Peel kiwifruit and quarter each fruit.

Peel and pit peaches, then cut each into 8 pieces. Pit and quarter plums. Peel bananas and cut into long thin slices. On a large platter or dish, arrange selection of fruit decoratively. Serve immediately with hot or cold mango sauce.

Makes 8 servings.

Total calories: 1438   Total fat: 13 g
Calories per serving: 180   Fat per serving: 2 g

LEMON-CHEESE TART

1 cup graham cracker crumbs
3 tablespoons reduced-fat margarine, melted
1 tablespoon unflavored gelatin powder
3 tablespoons water
2/3 cup light whipping cream
1-1/4 cups nonfat yogurt
1/2 cup low-fat cream cheese
1/4 cup sugar
Grated peel and juice of 2 lemons
Lemon slices and mint sprigs, to decorate

In a bowl, stir together crumbs and margarine. Press mixture over bottom of an 8-inch loose-bottomed tart pan. Refrigerate 30 minutes.

In a small bowl, sprinkle gelatin over 3 tablespoons water. Set aside 2 to 3 minutes to soften. Stand bowl in a saucepan of hot water and stir until gelatin dissolves. Cool slightly. Into a blender or food processor, place cream, yogurt, cream cheese, sugar, lemon peel and juice and gelatin. Blend until smooth and well mixed.

Pour lemon mixture over crumb crust, smoothing surface. Cover and refrigerate until set. To serve, carefully remove from pan and place on a serving plate. Decorate with lemon slices and mint sprigs before serving.

Makes 8 servings.

Total calories: 1512   Total fat: 86 g
Calories per serving: 189   Fat per serving: 9 g

——ORIENTAL FRUIT PAVLOVA——

3 egg whites
3/4 cup sugar
Few drops vanilla extract
1/2 teaspoon white-wine vinegar
1 teaspoon cornstarch, sifted
1/2 cup light whipping cream
1/2 cup nonfat yogurt
12 ounces prepared fresh fruit, such as starfruit,
    lychees, mango, melon, dates, mangosteen

Preheat oven to 300F (150C). On a sheet of parchment paper, draw a 7-inch circle. Place paper, marked-side down, on a baking sheet. In a large bowl, beat egg whites until stiff.

Beat in half of the sugar, then, using a metal spoon, gently fold in remaining sugar, the vanilla, vinegar and cornstarch. Spread meringue over the circle on the paper, building sides up higher than the center. Bake 1 to 1-1/2 hours until meringue is crisp and dry. Cool on a wire rack, then carefully peel off the paper.

In a bowl, whip cream until stiff; gently fold in yogurt. Place meringue on a serving plate, pile cream mixture into the center and arrange prepared fresh fruit decoratively on top. Serve immediately.

Makes 8 servings.

Total calories: 1292   Total fat: 40 g
Calories per serving: 162   Fat per serving: 5 g

— STRAWBERRY-FILLED ROLL —

3 eggs
1/2 cup granulated sugar
3/4 cup all-purpose flour
1/4 cup unsweetened cocoa powder
1 tablespoon hot water
1 cup low-fat cream cheese, room temperature
1/4 cup reduced-sugar strawberry jam
6 ounces strawberries
1 tablespoon powdered sugar

Preheat oven to 400F (205C). Grease a 13″ × 9″ baking pan. Line with waxed paper and grease the paper. In a bowl, over a pan of hot water, beat eggs and granulated sugar together until thick, pale and creamy.

Remove bowl from heat and beat until mixture is cool. Sift flour and cocoa over egg mixture, add hot water and gently fold in. Pour mixture into prepared pan, tilt pan to level the surface. Bake 12 to 15 minutes until firm to touch. Turn out onto a sheet of waxed paper. Using a serrated knife, cut off crisp edges and roll up with paper inside. Let cool.

Unroll gently and spread with cream, then jam. Slice strawberries and place on jam, reserving a few for decoration. Roll up again and place on a serving dish. Sift powdered sugar over roll and decorate with reserved strawberry slices.

Makes 6 servings.

Total calories: 1501   Total fat: 31 g
Calories per serving: 250   Fat per serving: 5 g

—MELON WITH GINGER SAUCE—

1 small cantaloupe or honeydew melon
1 ounce crystallized ginger
2/3 cup ginger wine or ginger ale
1/4 cup chopped hazelnuts

Using a knife, cut melon in half. Remove seeds and using a melon baller, scoop out flesh. Place melon balls into a small bowl.

Chop crystallized ginger finely. Add to melon balls, along with ginger wine. Mix gently but well. Cover and refrigerate at least 2 hours, stirring occasionally.

Into 4 glass serving dishes, spoon melon balls and sauce. Sprinkle with chopped hazelnuts to serve.

Makes 4 servings.

Total calories: 715   Total fat: 18 g
Calories per serving: 179   Fat per serving: 4 g

Note: Nuts can be chopped more easily if they are fresh, warm and moist.

— APPLE & ALMOND STRUDEL —

1-1/2 pounds cooking apples
1 tablespoon lemon juice
1/2 cup raisins
1/4 cup packed brown sugar
2 teaspoons apple-pie spice
8 sheets filo pastry dough
1/4 cup reduced-fat margarine, melted
2 cups fresh bread crumbs
1/4 cup sliced almonds
2 tablespoons powdered sugar

Preheat oven to 375F (190C). Grease a baking sheet. Peel, core and slice apples. Into a bowl, put apple slices. Sprinkle with lemon juice. Mix in raisins, brown sugar and spice.

Place one sheet of pastry dough on a sheet of parchment paper. Brush lightly with melted margarine. Place another sheet of dough on top and continue layering all the sheets of dough on top of one another, brushing each one lightly with margarine. Sprinkle bread crumbs over dough, leaving a 1-inch border uncovered all around edges. Spread apple mixture over bread crumbs, then fold border edges over fruit mixture. With a long side toward you, using parchment paper, roll up strudel.

Carefully place strudel on greased baking sheet, seam-side down, shaping the roll into a horseshoe, if desired. Brush roll lightly with margarine and sprinkle with almonds. Bake about 40 minutes or until crisp and browned. Sift powdered sugar over strudel before serving. Serve hot or cold.

Makes 8 servings.

Total calories: 1974   Total fat: 44 g
Calories per serving: 247   Fat per serving: 5 g

-GLAZED BLUEBERRY TARTLETS-

1 cup graham cracker crumbs
2 tablespoons finely ground blanched almonds
1/4 cup packed brown sugar
1/4 cup reduced-fat margarine, melted
12 ounces blueberries
1/2 cup red-currant jelly
2 tablespoons water
Mint leaves, to decorate

In a bowl, mix together crumbs, almonds, sugar and melted margarine.

Press mixture into 12 greased deep muffin pans; refrigerate 1 hour. Carefully remove tartlet cases from pans. Pile blueberries into tartlet cases.

In a saucepan, melt red-currant jelly with water. Brush over blueberries to glaze. Sift powdered sugar over tartlets before serving, if desired. Decorate with mint leaves.

Makes 12 tartlets.

Calories per tartlet: 126   Fat per tartlet: 6 g

—SPICY RAISIN CHEESECAKE—

5 tablespoons reduced-fat margarine
1/4 cup packed brown sugar
1-2/3 cup rolled oats
1 cup low-fat cream cheese
3 eggs, separated
1 teaspoon apple-pie spice
1/4 cup all-purpose flour
1/2 cup half and half
Grated peel and juice of 1 lemon
1/3 cup granulated sugar
1/2 cup golden raisins
1 tablespoon powdered sugar

In a saucepan, melt margarine and brown sugar together over low heat.

Remove from heat and stir in oats; mix together well. Press mixture over bottom of an 8-inch loose-bottomed tart pan. Refrigerate until firm. Meanwhile, preheat oven to 325F (165C). Into a blender or food processor, place cream cheese, egg yolks, apple-pie spice, flour, half and half, lemon peel and juice and granulated sugar. Blend until smooth and well mixed. Transfer mixture to a bowl. Stir in raisins.

In a separate bowl, beat egg whites until stiff. Using a metal spoon, fold gently into cheese mixture. Pour over crust and level surface. Bake 1 to 1-1/2 hours until brown and firm to touch. Cool on a wire rack, then remove from pan. Place on a serving plate and refrigerate until ready to serve. Sift powdered sugar over cheesecake before serving.

Makes 10 servings.

Total calories: 2555   Total fat: 100 g
Calories per serving: 255   Fat per serving: 10 g

FRUIT-FILLED CAKE

4 eggs
1/2 cup granulated sugar
1 cup all-purpose flour
3/4 cup light whipping cream
1/4 pound black grapes
1/2 small cantaloupe melon
2 kiwifruit
1 tablespoon powdered sugar

Preheat oven to 375F (190C). Grease an 8-inch deep cake pan. Into a large bowl, put eggs and granulated sugar. Beat until thick, pale and creamy. Sift flour over mixture. Using a metal spoon, fold in gently.

Pour batter into prepared pan, tilting pan to level surface. Bake 25 to 30 minutes until firm to touch. Turn out of pan and cool on a wire rack. In a bowl, whip cream until stiff. Prepare fruit. Halve and seed grapes. Peel, seed and dice melon. Peel and slice kiwifruit. In a bowl, gently mix fruit together. To assemble cake, cut the cake horizontally into 3 layers. Place bottom slice on a serving plate, cut-side up. Spread one third of the cream over bottom, then arrange some fruit on top.

Place a sponge cake on top and spread this with another third of cream. Arrange fruit on top. Place remaining sponge cake slice on top, cut-side down. Spread or pipe remaining cream over top and arrange remaining fruit decoratively over cream. Sift powdered sugar over top. Serve immediately.

Makes 10 servings.

Total calories: 2147   Total fat: 90 g
Calories per serving: 215   Fat per serving: 9 g

INDEX